THE KEY POINT OF THIS BOOK . . .

"There are *many* ways to become relaxed and energized. Different techniques will work differently for different people, and may even work differently for the same person at different times. So treat this book as a smorgasbord, going from appetizers to desserts, in order, heavying up on whatever catches your special fancy. If you give yourself a session once a day, or even several times a week, you can virtually guarantee yourself positive inner change. You'll be more relaxed and have more energy, a freer mind, a happier soul, stronger passion —all the things that make life worth living."

—Lowell G. Miller

Meta-Calisthenics

Inner Exercise

by Lowell G. Miller

PUBLISHED BY POCKET BOOKS NEW YORK

META-CALISTHENICS:
Inner Exercise

POCKET BOOK edition published December, 1976

Illustrations by Laura Bernay.

Contents

Meta-
Calisthenics

Chapter One

Introduction

IN THE SAME WAY THAT ELECTRICITY CONTINU-
ously powers a light bulb when it is on, energy is
constantly flowing through us as long as we are alive.
It's another kind of energy—a biological energy.
When we're feeling good, strong, and happy, we have
a lot of it. When we're feeling low, depressed, and
tired, we have a low level of energy or are unable to
utilize what is within us.

When we feel tense, for example, it's not just a
question of "having a tense feeling." We are actually
tense. Our bodies are literally—physically—constricted. This constriction stops the flow of life-giving
energy, and eventually we become fatigued or physically or emotionally ill.

States of consciousness, which are a function of
energy level, are no less associated with the body
than with the mind (though we tend to perceive ourselves mostly mentally). And we can guide or lead

or enhance our energy consciousness by working through either soma (body) or psyche (mind).

In the methods to follow, which emphasize the somatic approach, we are after the development of a kind of inner physique. The inner physique—a hard thing to describe in words—is your body as it relates to your emotions, your mind, your creativity, and the level of your energy. It's your state of *being*, located in the body.

When you build the "muscles" of your inner physique, you will see visible changes in your outer body at the same time that you feel invisible changes in your inner one. Your energy will be more intense and smoother; you'll be more sensitive and sensuous, calmer, more relaxed and in charge of yourself. Your posture and walk are bound to change, your skin and eyes will brighten, your muscle tone will improve. As an inevitable side effect, the movement exercises, in combination with a more satisfied frame of mind, will slim you down. Your body will begin to seem like a new organism altogether—you'll feel like a caterpillar turning into a butterfly.

People have been engaged in the somatic approach to conscious development—increasing energy and awareness through physical techniques—at least since the beginning of recorded history. Long before our drug era of uppers and downers, tranquilizers and hallucinogens, there was a body of knowledge (among both primitive and civilized cultures) devoted to the improvement of the individual's state by safe and natural means.

Tibetan and Japanese Buddhists, Indian Yogis, Sufis in the Middle East, Gurdjieffians, Aricans, and Reichians in the West—all have devoted a great deal of effort to the discovery of methods that produce positive change. Consciousness development is a science and an art, and large principles and individual masters have contributed to the field, just as they have in the history of painting or poetry or physics. In this book you will find the cream of their efforts—in addition to discoveries of my own, modified to suit the needs of individuals in contemporary society. You don't have to speak Hindu or Japanese, and you don't have to believe in the magic powers of some strange Asiatic deity—all you have to believe is that energy is real.

This chapter covers principles and explanations that will affect your understanding of all the techniques, but without a little firsthand experience it will be just so much intellectualizing in a vacuum. So let's consider one very simple yet effective exercise as an example. It's called slow hand meditation. Read the instructions all the way through first, and then put this book aside and *do* it.

Sit yourself in a comfortable chair, arranged so that your backbone is fairly straight but not rigid. (If you want, you can also do this one lying down, flat on your back, no pillow, eyes on the ceiling.) Now open your eyes as wide as you possibly can and hold them there for a slow, silent count of ten (it's okay to blink). Then, when you've reached ten, slowly, ever so slowly let your eyelids drop, and finally close your eyes completely.

Your hand should be resting comfortably, palm up, on a flat surface (chair arm, thigh, bed). You can start off with either hand, since eventually you're going to perform the same actions with both.

With your eyes closed, just think about your hand for a minute. Try to feel all the muscles and sinews and bones; try to feel the weight of the atmosphere on the skin of your palm. As you think about your hand, become aware also of your breathing. In comes the good air—out goes the bad air.

Now, from the flat-palm-upward position, slowly, ever so slowly, begin to curl your thumb and forefinger toward each other (remember, eyes closed for this). The trick here is to do it *slowly,* as slowly as you possibly can while still moving. You want to curl both thumb and finger around until they make a closed circle, and the tips should touch *as lightly as possible.* The lighter the initial contact, the more effective this technique will be.

After you've touched thumb and forefinger, just as slowly return them to their original positions. Now do the same thing with each of your fingers in succession. After finishing one hand, move on to the other.

Don't forget: do it *slowly* and touch the fingertips *lightly.* That's what makes this work so well.

When you've finished slow hand meditation with both hands, inhale and exhale deeply, and gently lift your eyelids. Feel a little different?

In exercises such as slow hand meditation there are several elements operating that account for the final effect. These elements tend to be present in all the exercises in this book, so by analyzing a simple one we can get a good general understanding of a much larger range of techniques.

It's important to understand what the exercises are trying to do and why they work so that in the end you won't be tied to a set of printed instructions, but will be able to spontaneously create exercises that fit the special needs of your body.

There are two main types of exercises. The first, of which slow hand meditation is an example, seeks to generate new states of being by *reducing* the presence of or *negating* the old (normal) state of being. The second type involves an experimental search for new contents—new contents for the old state that has been emptied but will as surely as the seasons change want to fill itself again.

Let's concentrate first on the techniques that empty us out, that *relax* us, that relieve the frenzied buzzing of nervousness and break up the inner log jams of depression.

The idea behind working toward relaxation is simple. We need to be able to generate a relaxed state because the ordinary tensions under which we live inhibit and dissipate our energy. We unwittingly exhaust ourselves with fears, worries, anxieties, fantasies, and drives, all born of tension.

It's apparent that no one is totally and completely relaxed. Everyone is in one state of tension or another. In fact, you might say a person is *defined* by his or her level of tension. Anyone who could become absolutely and utterly relaxed would be a superbeing, and I don't think we can even *imagine* such a state. But in order for your state of being to change positively, toward expanded energy and perception, you have got to arrive at a lower-than-normal-for-you state of tension. Only at that point can the thoughts and gyrations of the mind that are the producers (and products) of tension begin to dissolve.

We can utilize physical techniques (or mental techniques, with the body as an indispensable aid) to take away these preoccupations. We can do it by teaching ourselves how to relax. We want to experience who and what we are when our thoughts and their cargo of tension are not controlling our lives. We want to clear our heads so that we can clearly feel ourselves —and our environment.

One-Pointedness

To do it, we need a set of techniques that will divert the mind from its normal preoccupation with thoughts. (Fantasies, schemes, calculations, memories, worries, responsibilities, hopes, fears—all are thoughts.) If we can divert the mind, we can empty it—at least temporarily. And if we can empty our minds we can be ourselves in a way that is utterly different and delightful.

One way to do it is to focus all our attention on a part of the body. The effect of this focusing is to wipe out all other thoughts and worries, and the further effect of such *nonintellectual concentration* is to produce in us a physical reduction in tension that will be accompanied by a feeling of relaxation and well-being. In slow hand meditation we did this by focusing our attention on the hand, and by moving the hand *slowly*. The extra difficulty of concentrating on moving slowly kept the mind from wandering.

This type of concentration on a single thing that eliminates other thoughts is called "one-pointedness," and it is a basic and necessary skill for the development of higher energy. There are lots of ways to focus yourself and gain one-pointedness—in transcendental meditation, for example, you are taught to become one-pointed by use of a mantra—but a quality all of them have in common is that it's a skill you *learn*. You have to apply yourself. It may be difficult at first, and you may never master it completely, but in your practical life and in your efforts to create a new internal energy state, the ability to attain a one-pointed state of intense concentration is absolutely invaluable.

The reason you felt refreshingly slowed down, quiet, alert, and somehow *changed* in your relationship to your surroundings after the slow hand meditation is that you achieved a temporary state of one-pointedness. This book contains at least a dozen methods for developing one-pointedness. Find one that suits you—attaining one-pointedness is a skill you've got to have.

Directing Mental Energy

Another aspect of slow hand meditation is the notion of "sending" your mind to a part of your body. You can't learn much about your body until you begin to pay attention to it, to examine what's there, to feel it. Most people have a rather hazy sense of how their own bodies feel from the inside. Because they are strangers to themselves, they don't even know where they are tense. When their bodies have a subtle emotional reaction to something, they can feel it, but they don't know where it is. If you *can* tune in to your body enough to feel it responding to your life, you can know who you are and how you feel despite destructive illusions and self-deceptions you may hold in your mind.

And if you can learn to send your mind into your body you can actually relax isolated parts of it with the power of your mind alone—give your inner physique an inner massage. This book will help you experience consciousness as something that flows, is everywhere, and can be *guided*, and is not just an aimless mass of energy trapped inside your brain.

Slow Motion

An important feature of slow hand meditation that will appear in many somatic exercises is the idea of *slowness*. By slowing down, we gain time to become aware of the processes that are going on in our bodies (and minds). The effect is very much like watching a slow-motion film—in this different time frame our perceptions are greatly intensified and refined.

Our lives are lived too fast today, and that's one of the reasons we've become so separated from our natural states of being and our more "primitive" direct lines of contact with true reality, with ourselves. Slowing down is a way of getting back—back to what we really are. It's a way of recovering our natural sensory awareness, our balance, and the kind of free-flowing energy all of us experienced as children. Slowness illuminates our current state of being by showing us a contrast. A slow and conscious body, a calm mind—these are rarities in the current world, and a brief experience of them can show us how we really *are* underneath our travail, can give up heightened consciousness.

We need to see ourselves if we are to grow. The human way of seeing is by comparison, by understanding contrasts and opposites. We don't pay any attention to black unless we are aware that there is such a thing as white. We make a distinction between lust and love because we know they are two different states. Air is air because it is not earth and not water and not fire. Speed, our most consciousness-deadening quality, becomes apparent when we intentionally experience what life is like when it is slower.

Breathing

There were two objects of attention in slow hand meditation. One was the hand; the other was breathing. Air is the single most important elemental need of a human being, and breathing is the most important feature of almost every method of awareness development. All around the globe, from the oldest Chinese systems to the most modern biofeedback trainings, breathing is recognized as the key to creating a unified and harmonious mind-body organism.

Our breathing always reflects our mental state. When we are tense and nervous our breathing is short, choppy, shallow, rapid. When we are relaxed, our breathing is slow, even, smooth, long, and deep. And because of the interdependence of body and state of being, we can *become* relaxed by consciously breathing as if we were in a relaxed state.

Breathing is a distinctly regular, repetitive, and tactile phenomenon. Merely by holding our attention on it we can be calmed in a hypnotic, highly internalized way. And there is a curious aspect of holding your attention on your breathing that you will notice right away. Without any effort on your part, without your actually trying to slow it down, your breathing will *automatically* slow down when you become one-pointedly aware of it. The corollary, of course, is that by becoming aware of your breathing you will relax.

It is a simple secret, but invaluable in daily life.

Wherever you are, whenever you feel your thoughts taking control of your mind or feel that you're losing your ability to cope, just take a little time out to become mindful of your breathing. You needn't try to alter it—just become aware of it. Try it now, for a few minutes.

In addition to helping you gain some control over your emotional state and the level of your energy, slower respiration slows your heartbeat and lowers your blood pressure. It makes a lot of sense that in the process of getting high naturally you are also taking important steps to improve and insure your physical health. No doubt there are other, as yet undiscovered, beneficial side effects.

Remembering Yourself

Gurdjieff, a great teacher of many methods for conscious development, articulated the concept of *remembering yourself*. When you focus your attention on your hand, you are in effect *remembering* it. When you focus on your breathing, you are remembering that you are constantly and always a breather. When you empty your mind of the noise of thoughts and worries, you are remembering that you are never without the potential for that state of psychophysical peace—it is there all the time, needing only to be revealed and realized . . . needing only to be remembered.

Talking about "remembering yourself" is another, more concrete way of talking about self-awareness. Perhaps our biggest problem in life, in terms of gaining and maintaining a pleasurable and intelligent state of being, is that we become so involved with our social context—job, family, ambitions, objects, anxieties, old wounds—that we actually *forget* we are feeling individuals. Our energy gets bottled up in our heads, and we constantly try to think our way out of situations for which thinking can only be a way *in* and not a way out (take sexual problems, for example). We forget our bodies. We forget our feelings, our real feelings. We become flotsam on a sometimes calm, sometimes violent emotional sea that is always beyond our control.

Worst of all, we forget to see ourselves. We forget to observe ourselves thinking; we forget to feel ourselves feeling. It is the awareness of self—the real, gut, direct awareness of self, the tangible and tactile awareness of self—that is the foundation for inner pleasure and inner change.

Try this exercise for instant insanity. Look around the room. Note every single thing you see. For each notation, say to yourself, "I am seeing this or that." Do it for everything you hear. Or smell. Or touch. Do it for the fact that you're sitting. Say to yourself as you read this, "I am reading this." *Try to be aware of everything you are doing.* Then you'll see how easy it is to forget, to be unconscious. When we remember ourselves—when we remember that we exist and exist in a fantastic complexity—then we exist all the more. Then we *are*. Z'hadi said, "Never forget . . . yourself."

Armor and the Flow of Energy

When our senses expand we perceive the One.
When our senses contract we perceive the Division.
—WILLIAM BLAKE

Some of the exercises in this book are intended to dispel nervous energy and slow down our overactive verbal minds. Others have as their purpose the production of energy when we are in the strangulating grip of that other form of anxiety, depression.

Nervousness and depression are relative. One or the other (or both, alternately), may be your normal state, and you may not even think of yourself as nervous or depressed. That's why the exercises in this book can make you feel better even if you feel okay to begin with. These exercises can improve skills in one-pointedness, self-consciousness, or concentration —and all, with greater emphasis on some techniques than on others, work to break down or dissolve what Wilhelm Reich called *body armor* so as to permit a free and natural flow of energy in the body.

For those unacquainted with Reich and with his style of thinking, I want to say that I am introducing nothing really new. The idea that there is energy in the body and that it can flow poorly or well is not at all an eccentric one outside the West; it appears in the classical thought of Japan, China, India, Tibet. Even here we acknowledge the existence of alpha and other waves—*waves of energy* actually being transmitted around and out of the body.

Reich, a biologist, psychiatrist, and renegade student of Freud who was part genius and part madman, articulated in Western terms the notion of a biological life force that animates us. The force—he called it orgone energy; the Yogis call it Prana; in Zen it is Ki, and for the Chinese, Chi—flows freely through our bodies in a natural state, but it is perverted and blocked by muscular traumas (contractions), traumas caused by socialization in infancy. We're taught to sit still; we're taught not to touch, not to embrace.

When we are *shamed* over some matter we feel it with a contraction in our bodies. The effort involved in restraining ourselves from doing things that we naturally yearn to do creates muscular and nervous rigidity and intractability. Our social inhibitions become internalized, frozen into our bodies, and there they remain.

Now, as we enter into this adult, "uptight" contracted world of physical tension, we each develop our own weirdly distorted and crippled body—for when we are tense in a certain place (e.g., jaws or stomach), the energy that is constantly flowing through our bodies like an invisible blood *cannot pass through* that place. That part of us begins to lose feeling—to die—and to upset the balance among all our other parts. Soon another part freezes up, and then another. Pretty soon our patterns are set. We stop growing. We become thick-skinned, tough-faced, stiff-bodied caricatures of the loose and creative animal the human was long ago born to be.

I've included many exercises in this book that break down or dissolve "armor," the energy blockages. Gaining increased energy means liberating the potential energy already existing in our bodies. It's like urban renewal for the individual.

In understanding the reasons for the exercises that follow, this is the most important point: *We alter our minds by altering our bodies, because "mind" and "body" are both the resulting functions of a single energy—a single energy that animates all organic life.* It's this energy that makes the difference between living things and dead things. It can be blocked and it can be freed, it can be perverted and it can be natural. We can control our destinies—change ourselves and our lives—to the extent that we can become intimate with and can influence our energy.

Until we realize that tension, for example, is not just an emotion or a clogging of our intellectual computers but a *total, physically grounded state*, we can't begin to deal with the negative forces that diminish us.

The exercises that follow—which should probably not be called exercises, really, for they are more like conduits for feeling yourself—relieve the kinds of contraction and blocked energy created by emotional tension in a direct, physical way. I have also included techniques for relaxing the mind, because that is the other path to self-evolution, and the two paths intertwine and need each other if either is going to work properly. A liquid body, a mind as cool and open as outer space—these are the night and day of consciousness.

When you're loose, when you can relax your body and empty your mind at will, you can really go places. You can see the world around you objectively, with a clear head, because you're less entangled with it and less influenced by it than you used to be. (You can see *yourself* objectively, too). A leaf or a blade of grass can become the most beautiful thing in existence. The air shimmers. Your face feels like flowing silver. You can feel something new in your palm. You're more loving and more able to be loved. It's energy, your connection with energy.

Chapter Two

The Attitude of Discovery

THE WAY TO BENEFIT MOST FROM THE INFORMA-
tion in this book is to be as open as possible to your
feelings. Be a kind of discoverer—an explorer, an
adventurer. Expect the unexpected. You can never
know in advance which methods will work best for
you, or even how they will work, so you've got to
remain open.

Openness has two main characteristics—avoidance
of strain, and trying not to interfere with your experience. This means trying not to *control* what happens, trying not to limit or establish boundaries.

You can't change or generate energy by gritting
your teeth and saying, "I will, I will." Why try to
smash through the walls of a house when, if you take
a little time, you can find the open door? In the
famous words of the Bhagavad-Gita:

> Cease striving;
> Change will come.

Take it easy on yourself, don't force things. Feeling, not force, is what will help you develop.

The human organism, like any other, *wants* to grow. If you open yourself to this growth and permit it, without decreeing it or insisting upon it, it will occur spontaneously. Few people are prepared to relinquish control of themselves even for an instant to permit free, spontaneous, undirected growth to take place. But it's what you *need* to do. For you must discover what is in you, where your energy is, how much you may have. You can't know what's there until you discover it directly.

To discover all that is possible, you also need to keep yourself from analyzing your experiences *while you are having them*. When you approach an experience analytically, it is almost impossible to *have* that experience. You drain off too much energy into your brain. In a sense, the whole point of this book is to learn to avoid that. If you analyze while practicing a technique, you will never get to have the experience you were trying to analyze. Think about "explanations" afterwards, if you must, but never before or during. Now, take off your thinking cap and stay awhile. . . .

Although this book contains instructions for many exercises—"recipes" that will relax and energize you —much emphasis must be placed on your own style of doing things. After you have learned the techniques in this book you can be creative with them and shape your activities to your own special body and needs.

There is a stage beyond this, too, in which you'll begin to invent and discover methods that are *yours,* just as a jazz musician invents complex and personal music from a basic simple tune. At this stage you'll have learned how to feel your armor, and you'll be able to teach yourself how to release it.

To get from stage one (following instructions and discovering) to stage two (creative modification) to stage three (improvisation) you need to teach yourself how to "go with the flow" of natural processes. This means you have to overcome, to some extent, a culturally conditioned anxiety about organic life processes and spontaneous functioning. When you first begin to tap your repressed reservoirs of energy, things will happen that will surprise you.

Sometimes you may find that a certain posture causes you to begin spontaneous heavy breathing; perhaps you'll even find yourself hyperventilating. This is not something to be afraid of. This is your body taking over and taking what it wants, what it has not gotten for a very long time. You've finally done something to free your body, to wake it up.

You may feel other signs, more frightening ones— nausea, dizziness, uncontrollable yawning, anger, muscle pains. Unless you have been straining (which you are constantly advised not to do), these are also signs of the awakening of the body and emotions. Often you are retrieving intense emotional experiences you once had that you felt forced to repress and that ultimately shut you down. When these manifestations occur, just relax. Concentrate on your breathing; breathe slowly and deeply. Don't try to make the signs go away. Recover your equilibrium slowly, and as you do so, try to discover *what the experience means for you*, what it relates to in your past or in your attitudes to life.

Other things you may experience are hot and cold sweats, feelings of heat or coldness, pin-prick pains, crying, magnification of pulse, coughing, spitting, farting, coolness or roaring in the ears, opening or closing of the sinuses, sudden sharpness of vision, anxiety symptoms such as headache and stomach cramp, tingling sensations, streaming sensations (as if a liquid were flowing within you), rhythmic "magnetic" circling feeling within the body or certain parts of the body, physical "hollow" feelings, lightheadedness, and hallucinations.

Obviously some are pleasure feelings—these you should try to allow to continue, you should keep doing —gently—whatever caused them. Some are unpleasure feelings—these you should try to clarify in your mind, but you should not try to force them away. Both are the results of awakening your dormant energy and your dormant self. Pleasure is the real you; unpleasure is what you sometimes have to go through to get there. They are both the body's natural way of revivifying itself, and the best thing you can do is to avoid interfering.

Relinquish control to natural healing processes— that's one of the surest pathways to inner growth. Stand aside for a moment and see what your Self will do for itself if you leave it alone. It wants to live. *Let* it live!

Chapter Three

Breathing

THOUGH THE EASTERN SCHOOLS OF CONSCIOUS-ness intuitively understood the need for proper breathing, we needn't be satisfied by an intuition or belief. Our own experience shows us the intimate connection between breathing and emotional state. And a quick course in respiratory anatomy will show us how breathing relates to the health and total functioning of our bodies on the most basic organic levels.

Take a minute to examine the illustration of the respiratory and circulation systems so you'll have a good concrete image of what's happening as I describe it.

Air is drawn into the lungs by the action of the diaphragm, a strong, sheetlike muscle that is stretched across the chest, separating the chest-box from the abdomen. The diaphragm's action is usually automatic (as the heart's is), but we can "operate" it manually through conscious awareness, and we can improve the quality of its ordinary automatic opera-

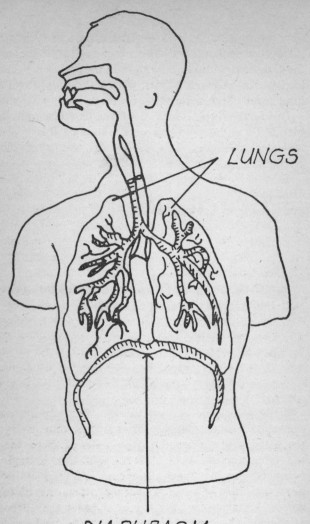

LUNGS

DIAPHRAGM
(Lungs grow larger as it
pulls downward)

tion by practice, as with any other muscle. When the diaphragm expands, or when we expand it, it increases the size of the chest and lungs. This creates a vacuum into which fresh air rushes. When the diaphragm relaxes, the chest and lungs contract, and we exhale.

Inside the lungs, oxygen makes contact with our blood. To understand the implications of this process, we need to digress briefly into the matter of blood circulation.

Driven by the heart, blood is pumped through the arteries to every part of the body, which it vitalizes, nourishes, and strengthens. The blood then returns to the heart, which pumps the used blood for "recharging" to the lungs. More than anything the blood is a carrier of oxygen, and it must constantly be purified and refreshed.

Blood starts on its arterial journey bright red and rich, laden with life-giving properties. It returns by the veins poor, blue, and dull, laden down with the waste of the system, used up. This used blood goes to the right ventricle of the heart; from there, it is sent to the lungs, where it is distributed by millions of hairlike blood vessels to the air cells that line the lungs.

Upon inhaling, oxygen comes into contact with the used (tired!) blood through the thin walls of the hairlike blood vessels. (The walls of these vessels are thick enough to hold blood but thin enough to allow oxygen to penetrate them.) A kind of combustion occurs when the oxygen contacts the blood—the blood takes up oxygen and releases the carbonic acid gas, CO_2, generated from the waste products and poisonous matter that have been gathered up by the blood from all parts of the system. Purified and oxygenated, life-giving blood then makes another trip

31

through the body. In twenty-four hours, your body recycles the equivalent of 35,000 pints of blood!

But if you don't get enough fresh air into your lungs, your blood cannot be sufficiently oxygenated or purified. Waste products that should have been destroyed are returned to circulation and poison the system. Imagine what would happen if the filtration system for your town's water supply suddenly broke down. Everyone would begin to take chemicals and dissolved metals into their systems, a little at a time. Slowly their bodies would weaken, their minds. . . .

The blood of a person who breathes improperly is, of course, of a bluish, dark color, lacking the rich redness of pure arterial blood. This often shows itself in a poor complexion. Proper breathing and good circulation result in a clear, bright complexion.

In imperfect or shallow breathing, only a portion of the lung cells are brought into play, and the system suffers in proportion to the degree that blood is under-oxygenated.

The lower animals, in their native states, breathe naturally. Primitive man undoubtedly did too. But the tense, rigid, mechanical life-style of "civilization" has robbed us of our natural habit of breathing, and we have suffered physically as well as psychically. When the importance of breathing has become clear to us there is only one option—corrective, remedial measures.

Starting from that most basic standpoint—proper physiological functioning—the techniques of breathing hold for us the promise of better health. And they hold a further promise—sensuous and spiritual pleasures totally unknown to those for whom breathing remains unconscious.

Deep and Complete Breathing

There are two types of wrong, inefficient breathing, and two types from which you get a lot of air for your effort. The types to avoid are "high" or "shoulder" breathing—raising your shoulders and breathing up high, at the base of the throat—and the very common "middle" breathing—expanding your chest by pushing out your ribs. It's amazing how often chest breathing is portrayed in our culture as the way to "take a breath of fresh air," because it's all wrong. When you expand your chest to breathe (and to do only that), you use only about half the capacity of your lungs.

The two right ways to breathe are to take the "deep" or "low" breath and the "complete" breath. Before you can do the complete breath (which is low, middle, and high breathing in one flowing motion), you have to master the deep breath.

Many singing teachers have exhorted their students to breathe through their stomachs. Now we all know that only the strangest mutant human could breathe through its stomach, but at least the singing teachers were on the right track. The idea is to expand your diaphragm (which most definitely is *not* your stomach) and increase the capacity of your lungs from below. In the process you're going to wind up stretching and loosening a lot of body armor below the belt. In fact, most people don't breathe deeply (and naturally) precisely because of this armor created by anxiety—sexual and otherwise. Diaphragmatic breathing may cause sexual excitement when you start out. Don't worry; it's perfectly normal. You haven't had your share of blood down there in *years*.

33

The diaphragm covers the abdomen in an arc and protrudes up into the chest organs like a hill. When the diaphragm is brought into action it lowers and distends the abdomen, pressing it down and away. The space thus vacated allows the lungs to expand. The lower lungs are allowed to fill only when the diaphragm is expanded—this is the *only way* air can enter the important depths of the lungs. In "low" breathing your stomach appears to swell down and out. This is actually the action of the diaphragm.

Though low (or deep, or abdominal) breathing is far superior to middle and high breathing in terms of total air and oxygen intake, it's not as good as what Yogis call the "complete breath." You should try to use the complete breath whenever possible. The idea is to get the most benefit from the least energy and to fill the *entire* lung space. That's what it's there for.

This doesn't mean you have to "stuff yourself" with air, but that you should do low, middle, and high breathing in a single smooth motion, so that the entire inner surface of the lungs will be exposed to fresh air.

The Complete Breath

After you've practiced low breathing, you're ready to work on the complete breath. Stand or sit erect—an erect posture allows free expansion of the lungs. Breathing through the nostrils, inhale steadily. First fill the lower parts of the lungs by distending the diaphragm (your stomach should swell from the groin up). Then fill the middle of the lungs by pushing out—in this order—the lower ribs, breastbone, and lower chest. Then fill the high space by protruding your chest and raising your shoulders. In this final movement the lower part of the abdomen will draw in slightly, giving the lungs support and helping to fill the high space.

At first you will find yourself making three or more distinct movements. You want to strive, though, for a uniform continuous inhalation—avoid the jerkiness that comes from overstuffing yourself with air in the beginning. As you practice, your muscles will stretch, you'll take in more air, and you'll get an interesting sensuous pleasure from the expansion.

Once you've inhaled, retain the breath as long as you comfortably can. As long as you've got the air in there, you might as well get the most out of it.

To exhale, slowly contract and raise the abdomen, then the middle area, then the high area. First in, first out. Try not to exhale in a great whoosh as if you'd been swimming under water. Do it slowly. Ideally, your exhale will be so gentle and subtle that you won't even hear the air passing out. (This comes after a bit of practicing, of course.)

It's important to exhale as fully as possible. Remember that the exhale is a way of taking waste products out of the body. Let your chest and diaphragm collapse a little bit, to squeeze out all the "bad" air.

The complete breath obviously generates health by increasing the oxygen level of your blood and aiding in the expulsion of waste products. It has other, more subtle, benefits as well. As the diaphragm contracts it exerts a gentle pressure on the liver, stomach, sex organs, and other organs. Its motion stirs the important organs of nutrition and elimination, massages and kneads them at each inhalation and exhalation.

It forces blood into them and squeezes it out, creating a kind of inner exercise that's just as important as outer exercise is for your muscles. Furthermore, the expansion of your abdomen and chest helps stretch and loosen body armor, which has a tendency to be particularly influential in the belly and breast areas. The constant expansion will help increase the size of your chest, too, if that interests you.

Try to do at least fifteen minutes a day of conscious complete breathing. You can do it anywhere—in a car, at your desk, in the bath, even while reading. If you persevere your conscious practice should eventually lead to the use of complete breathing as your ordinary mode of respiration. The transfer from conscious practice to unconscious habit can be slow, but it is well worth working toward. The next time you see an infant not yet trammeled by our hard-driving world, watch it breathe. That's the complete breath, the kind we were born with.

Breathing Exercises

The following breathing exercises should be done sitting or standing erect. If you sit, sit on the edge of your seat to avoid slumping on the chair back. There are other exercises that involve complicated postures or movements, but right now we are focusing on the classical methods for concentrating on breathing and breathing only. You will find that each exercise is also a form of light meditation—in each, your mind will be completely occupied with the system of breathing you are practicing.

The complete breath is the most important exercise, of course, and you should practice that one if nothing clse. The techniques below have been found effective for various purposes over thousands of years of testing. Some get you high, some calm you, some are intended to produce sweet voices or even psychic powers. You can choose which you want to do based on your needs, but it would be a good idea to test each one on yourself at least once. You can't tell merely from reading how a technique is going to *feel* for you, and the feeling is the important thing.

The Yogic Cleansing Breath

This exercise is often used as a conclusion to the practice of other breathing techniques, for its effect after a strenuous physical exertion is both restful and refreshing. It can also make you warmer if you're chilled.

1. Inhale a complete breath, slowly and fully.
2. Retain the air a few seconds.
3. Pucker up your lips as if to whistle, and then give a short, sharp exhale, as if you were blowing out a single candle. Stop for a moment, still retaining air, and then exhale the same way again. Continue until you have completely emptied your lungs. Then repeat the exercise. At first, ten repetitions should give you the desired effect. You should exhale about ten times for each repetition, but this will vary with your lung capacity.

The Energy Breath

This is a "feelgood" technique that will bring you energy immediately, and if you practice it over a period of time, your normal energy level will increase greatly. Your highs will be higher and your lows much less low and less frequent. The energy breath stimulates your entire nervous system, and is terrific to do upon rising in the morning—it's got less protein but far more power than an entire box of Wheaties.

1. Stand erect.

2. Inhale a complete breath and retain.

3. Extend your arms straight out in front of you (still retaining the breath) with only enough force to hold them out—don't flex your muscles.

4. Continuing to retain your breath, slowly draw your hands back toward your shoulders. As you do so, gradually make fists and increase the muscle pressure in your arms. By the time you reach your shoulders your fists will be tightly clenched and you will be able to feel the vibration of the muscles in your arms.

5. *Still* retaining your breath, push the fists *slowly* out. Then draw them back *rapidly*, smacking into your shoulders. Do this five times.

6. Exhale vigorously through the mouth.

7. Repeat as many times as you comfortably can.

8. Do the Yogic cleansing breath.

9. Sit or stand quietly and feel the energy you have generated.

The key here is extreme tension in the muscles and a *rapid* drawing back of the fists. Obviously, you need the deepest possible breath in order to do it. This is one of those exercises that you might start feeling a little silly about doing—after all, the motions are so strange—but try to give the benefit of the doubt and simply focus on what you're doing. The method will prove itself overwhelmingly.

The Yogic Vocal Breath

No one is really sure why it works, but over thousands of years and for thousands of Yogis this simple exercise has resulted again and again in a sweeter and more melodious voice. A nice voice isn't exactly the prime requisite for improving consciousness, but it will probably make you feel better about yourself.

1. Inhale a complete breath as slowly as you can, through the nostrils (as always).

2. Retain the air.

3. Expel the air vigorously in one great breath through a wide open mouth—as wide as you can get it.

4. Repeat several times.

5. Do the Yogic cleansing breath.

Chest Expansion

We spend most of our waking time sitting. Since almost no one sits perfectly erect, the chest cavity in most of us has been collapsed by the slumped posture in which we ordinarily sit. Clearly, the lungs cannot expand fully if the cavity they occupy has decreased in volume and will not let them. This exercise is very good for restoring natural lung space and giving chest expansion.

1. Stand erect.

2. Inhale a complete breath.

3. Retain the air.

4. Extend both arms forward. Clench both fists and hold them together, arms fully extended in front of you, on a level with the shoulders.

5. Draw the fists back vigorously until the arms stand out straight sideways from the shoulder as if you were playing airplane.

6. Return your arms to position 4 and repeat step 5.

7. Exhale vigorously through an open mouth.

8. Do the Yogic cleansing breath.

Only repeat this exercise a few times in one session —it can give you a Charley horse if you overdo it.

A variation is to try to inhale a little more air when your arms are spread in position 5; this will expand the chest still further.

Chest Expansion Number Two

1. Clasp your hands in front of you at chest level, elbows facing outward.

2. Raise elbows as high as possible on each side of your head, allowing your clasped hands to rise to the chin. As you do this, inhale deeply.

3. Lower elbows until they touch the ribs. As you do this exhale completely.

4. Repeat.

As you raise your elbows up, your whole upper torso should flow up with them. Even try to stretch your head and neck upward in this movement.

A Breathing/Meditation Exercise to Do While Walking

You don't necessarily have to take time out of your day in order to reap the benefits of proper breathing and the relaxation and energy that it brings. And if you do this exercise, you'll get a rather different sense of your body and the environment you're walking through—which is largely composed of . . . air.

Keep your eyes facing forward; avoid fixing your gaze on any one particular thing. Walk with your head up, your chin tucked in slightly, your shoulders back.

1. As you walk, inhale a complete breath, counting silently from one to six, one count to each step, spreading the inhalation over six counts.

2. Now exhale on a count of six, one step to each count.

3. Continue walking and breathe normally.

4. Repeat.

If you can, try to retain your breath for a count of six (or at least three) before exhaling.

Many people tend to walk in a great hurry—to make appointments on time, or because they're full of anxiety over what has just happened or what they imagine is *going* to happen. Do this walking exercise whenever you catch yourself speeding as a pedestrian. You'll see that living *doesn't* have to be so tense, so focused on things other than your own body and your own self.

Coming to Attention

Many practitioners of martial arts use breathing techniques as a way of rousing their strengths and concentrating their minds. This exercise is useful in developing a state of animate relaxation—that is, a state in which you're relaxed but alert—and is good to do in the morning before breakfast or prior to meditating.

1. Stand erect in a military attitude—head up, eyes front, shoulders back, knees stiff, the palms of your hands resting on your thighs. Keep your eyes open a little wider than normal, so you feel a little coolness under the lids.

2. As you inhale a full, deep, complete breath, slowly rise up on your toes, and at the same time raise your arms up in a great arc until the palms are facing skyward. If you like, also let your head drop gently backward on your neck.

3. Staying in this position, retain your breath for a count of five.

4. Slowly sink back to the starting position, exhaling through the nostrils.

5. Repeat several times, and then do the Yogic cleansing breath.

41

You can vary the technique by going up on one leg at a time, arching way backward at the top of the inhale, touching your toes when you come down on the exhale, or holding your hands in a taut claw shape (as if you were some primitive beast). The movement should be as graceful as you possibly can make it. This exercise is also called The Swan, or The Sea-Flower.

Alternate Nostril Breathing

This is a favorite of Yogis and Sufis, and is without a doubt the best natural tranquilizer known to man. You can do it anywhere, any time during the course of your day. It should definitely be in your repertoire of regular energy techniques. Alternate nostril breathing is to self-realization as cottage cheese is to dieting.

1. Sit comfortably, cross-legged or at the edge of your chair. Your back should be erect, but not rigid or straining. Close your eyes. Take a few complete breaths.

2. Close the right nostril with your right thumb and inhale through the left nostril. As you inhale, focus your attention a few inches below your navel and feel your abdomen expanding as your diaphragm pushes it out and away.

3. Now close the left nostril with your right finger. Remove your thumb and exhale through the right nostril.

4. When you have exhaled fully, inhale through the right nostril. Close it with the thumb, release the left nostril and exhale through it. This is a complete round. Continue this procedure for twenty rounds. Try to make your inhales and exhales as noiseless as possible, breathing carefully and slowly.

After you can do alternate nostril breathing without

making mistakes, add breath retention to the exercise. The rhythmic ratio should be one unit inhale to two units retention to two units exhale. You might start, for example, with a four-second inhale, eight seconds of retention, and an eight-second exhale. Keep in mind that the exact rhythm you use is not nearly as important as the fact that you *have* a rhythm. (This goes for all the breathing techniques.) Constant, steady, smooth, and repeating.

The Kundalini Breath of Fire

Before central heating, the bellows was a fireplace fixture, used to fan the fire into flame. Fire burns fuel, of course, as we burn food, but what it really needs to heighten its energy is air (and the oxygen air has in it). The metaphor holds for us; air gives us what we need to heighten our energy. There are some theories about a rather miraculous connection between air and energy that I'll discuss at the end of this chapter, but for now all you need to do is keep in mind the metaphor of a fire with wind fanning the flames.

While the fire has no choice in its circumstances and cannot generate oxygen at will, we do and we can. You come fully equipped with a bellows at no additional cost. Using it, you will find nothing that can stimulate circulation and clear the brain (blood goes there too, you know) better than the Kundalini Breath of Fire exercise. All you have to do is imagine that you're a smoldering bed of coals and that you're going to pump yourself into a raging blaze.

Always go through some of the other techniques— say, complete breathing, coming to attention, and alternate nostril breathing—before doing the Breath of Fire. You'll get much more out of it if you loosen up and focus on your system first.

1. Stand slightly bent from the waist, knees loose, hands resting gently on the thighs or the hips.

2. Inhale a complete breath through your nostrils.

3. Now pump the air out through your nostrils by sharply contracting the diaphragm.

4. Relax the diaphragm and inhale.

5. Quickly contract the diaphragm for a sharp exhale.

6. Repeat the inhales and exhales in rapid succession for twenty seconds to start; then increase the time period.

7. On your last inhale, take a complete breath. Retain it for ten seconds. Exhale slowly and return to normal breathing.

Concentrate on your exhales, on a sharp pumping out from the diaphragm. The inhales will take care of themselves, automatically. Noise is okay—you'll wind up sounding something like a locomotive. As you increase your skill, try for greater speed and depth of breath, and longer time periods. Try to find a posture that you can hold comfortably without jerking about as you practice this rather violent and potent technique. Remember, the exhale comes from the *diaphragm*.

The Total Exhale

The more completely you expel CO_2 and stale air from your lungs, the more room you're going to have for new air and oxygen. Exhaling is a form of cleansing the body, and the following method will make you squeaky clean. It also is the best technique for an "inner massage" of the vital abdominal organs, and it helps flatten your stomach.

The total exhale will stretch body armor that extends into the pelvic area, and, if you apply an anal lock—to do this, tighten your anus after you've exhaled—you'll massage your sex organs from within. The total exhale often gives me a mellow, relaxed, high feeling that I can't explain, except to say that it must loosen some armor I'm not even aware of.

1. Stand in a relaxed posture, slightly bent forward, as for the Breath of Fire.

2. Inhale a diaphragmatic breath of moderate volume.

3. Expel the air with great force by contracting your diaphragm.

4. Exhale as fully and completely as you can. *Do not* follow this with an inhale.

5. Keeping your abdomen in an inverted position, contract the diaphragm still further—pull it up and backward, toward the heart and spine. Pull in as deeply as you can, and up as hard as you can.

6. Hold the raised position for *at least* a count of five.

7. Relax the diaphragm and abdominal muscles; then inhale, return to normal breathing, and rest.

8. Repeat.

9. Do this at least five times to start, gradually building up your ability for more repetition.

10. Follow with the cleansing breath or complete breath.

The Principles Behind Proper Breathing

Those who teach breathing often like to make of it something mysterious and complex. As in meditation, one often hears that *only* this way or *only* that way is the correct way to breathe. Of course, the "right" way always turns out to be the speaker's own particular choice.

The exercises I've outlined in this chapter come from many disciplines and are practiced in modified forms by people interested in mind expansion, mind control, physical development, and relaxation. You can, to be sure, simply follow the instructions I've given, and you will have techniques enough to last you all your days. (None of these exercises are "beginning" or "advanced," really. The level of your progress is measured only by how carefully, smoothly, and one-pointedly you are able to do them.)

To be certain that you will come to a breathing method that you really like and can embrace totally (so you can be enjoying it and not "exercising" yourself), you need to understand the few simple principles that flow through all the methods. When you understand these, you can modify or invent techniques to suit yourself without losing any of the benefits of proper breathing.

Inhaling

Except when practicing one or two rare methods that will appear later in this book, always inhale through the nostrils. They're there for a purpose. The cilia in the nose catch dust and floating organisms that would otherwise contaminate your lungs. The nasal passages also serve to warm the air, so the difference between the temperature of the outer air and your inner organs will not be too great or shocking. And, inhaling through the nostrils tends to create a long, slow, even draw—one that you can *feel* better and become more aware of, which is usually what you're after.

Retention

Quite logically, you get the most benefit from your energy by *retaining* after you've inhaled. The oxygen you've taken in has more chance to be absorbed into the bloodstream; the CO_2 has more chance to be released. If you believe that the air contains an energy, Ki or Chi or orgone or Prana, there's a larger opportunity to absorb it if you retain your breath. The principle is basically economical—try to get as much nourishment as you can from every breath.

The exception here is rapid breathing, as in the Breath of Fire. You make up for not using all the air by taking in much more new air in the same period of time.

Fullness

Your inhale and exhale should nearly always be as full and deep as possible. The reasons for this have already been discussed. You should do some form of complete breathing at least once a day.

The Diaphragm

The diaphragm is the key to proper breathing and the one most people are going to have trouble with. Your diaphragm is probably going to be tight and inelastic at first, and your coordination is liable to be poor. But this goes away with practice, and when it does you can get a lot of sensuous pleasure merely from a deep inhale. (Remember that the diaphragm is also your third hand for the massage of inner organs.)

Rhythm

You must have noticed that all the exercises had a rhythm for inhale, retention, and exhale. Exactly what a proper rhythm is is a matter of opinion. The Yogis have one idea, Sufis another, Buddhists still another, and there are disagreements even among practitioners of the same sect. The point to remember, though, is that you *must* have a regular and repeating rhythm.

The rhythm should be one that can be expressed in a ratio. Some examples used by Yogis and Sufis follow. (Count by seconds or by heartbeats.)

Inhale		Retention		Exhale
1	to	2	to	2
1	to	4	to	4
4	to	8	to	6
4	to	6	to	8
4	to	12	to	8

The ratio you choose should be one that is comfortable and at the same time extends you somewhat (but *don't strain*). You need one that you can handle without feeling that it has to be "the best," but one that will nevertheless help you grow. If your rhythm is too easy you'll lose much of the power attainable through breathing; if it's too hard, you'll be tense, striving, and unable to concentrate. This latter condition is precisely what consciousness techniques strive to avoid!

Concentration

Every form of consciousness breathing is a way of removing you from your limiting and anxiety-producing concerns. You shouldn't do it as you might watch TV while preparing dinner. You should give yourself to it fully, even if you're doing it while stuck in a traffic jam or on a crowded subway.

Become aware of the air entering you, filling you. Feel the expansion and contraction of your diaphragm, the effects of it on your muscles. Feel where you're tight, where you're loose. In a word, *concentrate* on what you're doing. As I mentioned in the first chapter, concentration on rhythmic physical sensation is one of the most basic forms of meditation. Remember that when you breathe, you're not just breathing—you're walking down the long stairway to your inner caverns. Always try to relax more and more with each exhale.

Creating Your Own Breathing Techniques

Now that you have a repertoire of time-tested methods and an understanding of the principles underlying them, there's no reason you can't begin to modify them to suit your own needs or even "grow your own." When I say you can bend the rules, though, I only mean to say that the rules can be flexible—I don't mean that you should feel free to duck out and forget some important aspect merely because it's awkward or difficult for you in the beginning. You've got to learn the standard exercises first.

When you can see and feel what's happening as you breathe, you can begin to think more about your own special body—on which you are the world's greatest expert. You'll see when we get into poses and movements that the breathing exercises are important *per se*. Beyond that, however, you'll see that they're also something like musical scales. Once you've practiced them and incorporated them into your body, you'll be able to play around and invent some very interesting music. But if you don't learn them well you'll get nowhere when it comes to the real performance.

In goes the good air, out goes the bad air. . . .

Chapter Four

Still Life

IT'S OFTEN BEEN SAID THAT THE GREAT CONTRI-bution of Eastern philosophy has been the teaching that you can experience reality directly by just sitting still. For such a simple idea to be so potent seems rather shocking, but its basic truth is indisputable. And there are good reasons for its validity.

Underlying the importance of *stillness* to experience is what you might call the artichoke principle. To get to the sweet, rich heart of the artichoke you must peel away the many thorny surrounding leaves—each of which contains nourishment in only a fraction of its total size. In a person, the thorny leaves of personality, body armor, and circumstances must be peeled away before you can truly feel yourself and the space that you inhabit.

In ordinary life, your mind and your senses are constantly preoccupied. If we're not worried about the past we're worried about the future, and if we're not thinking of those two we're superimposing our anxieties upon the present. (Am I looking right? Am I acting right? Am I normal? Am I crazy? Can I get what I want?) Besides that, we have an ever-present navigation problem. Whenever we're *doing* something —whether it's walking, cooking, driving, reading— our organism has to be geared toward properly performing the task. No matter how internalized we may become while doing something else, our energy is always divided, never one-hundred percent devoted to *being*, to feeling ourselves, to tuning in to the forces in our environment.

What we're looking for in stillness is the chance to strip ourselves down to our metaphysical bones, down to the naked fact of our existence. We need to distance ourselves and minimize all but the fact that we exist. We need to start from scratch, as it were, with nothing, as a no one, to understand the layers and layers that have been heaped upon that originality —the layers, the leaves covering the heart, that block us off from ourselves, from the natural flow of our energy.

The techniques of still life have several specific purposes. The first, of course, is to slow you down, to give you a chance to go inside your body, to feel it, to feel yourself. When you do slow down, you become aware not only of how your body feels, but of what is going on in your mind. And you sensitize yourself to armor—you begin to make the connection between the way your body feels and what's going on in your mind. These two things, as you will see, are preparatory to and necessary for meditation. If you have armor that's causing obsessive thoughts to rule your mind, you've got to locate it and deal with it—otherwise the thoughts will persist.

You can't meditate by simply meditating. You've got to straighten out your body first. And to do that you need a way of examining it. The still-life techniques are the equivalent of stop-action television work; they can isolate events that happen almost too quickly to perceive.

When you are still, not *doing* things, your senses expand. Your hearing and sense of touch become more acute; your vision sharpens. The various qualities of space in your environment—form, line, color, volume, etc.—become more apparent, and they seem different from the way you normally perceive them. (It's crucial to be able to perceive the qualities of space as they really are. Space is what you live in.)

Still life is an identification method. You identify states; you identify armor (and neurosis), weakness and strength, the patterns of your personality—you identify the fact that you exist in an infinite universe. This is the most basic and crucial fact of all.

In each of the following techniques, try to let your body talk to you. Send your mind around to every part of your body as you hold a pose; look for stiffness, tension, and energy blocks. Listen to your body, and you will know what to work on. It wants to become loose and free-flowing, it really does; and if you are very still, very quiet—so quiet that you can hear sounds no ear has ever heard and feel things no finger has ever touched—your body will tell you what to do.

Yoga Postures

Yoga is the best-known physical path of awareness in the West, and with good reason. Anyone who practices it can see satisfying results almost immediately. It has numerous health benefits and was developed in an intuitive tradition specifically devoted to releasing the body from the lock-tight grip of the mind (and vice versa). Here we will deal with the most important postures. (There are many books on the subject if you want to go further with it.) Remember, as you read the instructions, that the *way* you do a pose is just as important as the fact that you *do* it. Don't try to compete with yourself and do it perfectly if you're stiff at first—it's amazing how much you'll loosen up and stretch out with practice. And never, never, never strain yourself. Work within your limits—they'll expand themselves. If you huff and puff and contort yourself trying to achieve a perfect posture, if your muscles vibrate with the effort, you will only be defeating yourself. In Yoga, you must always strive for grace of movement. Be mindful that the end-point is relaxation—psychophysical relaxation.

Many practitioners of Yoga claim that the best time to do it is in the morning. Most people, though, can't manage more than a hurried breakfast before they rush off to work or school. (My friends and I are lucky if we can find two socks of the same color.) So, without deprecating the vast experience of many adepts, I would suggest that the best time to practice Yoga is when *you* decide to do it. Late at night is probably *not* a good time, since your body will be fatigued, and you shouldn't do it right after eating. For many, I imagine, this is going to leave the time period before dinner, after you've arrived home. It's a good time to get rid of the stresses of the day, and to relax and revitalize yourself for the coming evening.

Whatever time you decide upon, try to keep it

regular. You needn't give yourself a full workout every day, but your body has a tendency to become more responsive if you practice at the same time of day. Of course, after you find out what Yoga's all about, you may want to do it instead of taking a coffee break, or practice during your lunch hour.

It's a good idea to practice Yoga outside, if possible. Air is important, since breathing techniques are an integral part of the postures. And, since you're striving for calm and relaxation, a peaceful outdoor environment is very helpful. But since most of us don't have access to outdoor space at the times of day available for Yoga, we'll have to make do inside. Be sure you have an open window nearby, though—fresh air is important.

Yoga is practiced on a hard surface, usually one covered with a rug. You won't take up much room, and even a towel can be enough to protect you from the floor. *Never, never* do Yoga on a bed. Whenever I've tried it I've gotten a week's worth of sore back muscles for my indulgence. For some postures a bed can be downright dangerous. It's tempting—sometimes you'll just be lying in bed and have the urge for a Yoga stretch—but *don't do it*.

Clothes should be loose-fitting, or, better, non-existent. (In most Yoga schools the women wear leotards and the men wear shorts.) All though this book you'll find methods directed toward getting you in touch with your body. Clothes inhibit the tactile sense, and anyway, as long as you're going to be getting in touch with your body you might as well take a look at it!

In Yoga there are four types of postures: relaxation poses, forward bending, backward bending, and the head-shoulder stands. These four types of postures, together, are enough to stretch and release every single muscle in your body. And they all have an uncanny simplicity—and an equally uncanny effectiveness.

Relaxation Poses

In Yoga, there must always be an interval between stretch postures for rest and relaxation. The body needs time to adjust to the effects of these stretches, since they are therapeutic and not merely "natural" poses. So the Yogis developed body positions that give full and complete rest. You can use them at other times too, when you just want to let your body rest.

The simplest is the **corpse pose.** To do the corpse pose, lie flat on your back, legs spread a foot or two apart. Rest your hands on the floor, palms up, next to your thighs. Close your eyes—look up to an imaginary point in the middle of your forehead, if you find that comfortable. Breathe deeply. Imagine your body getting heavier with each exhale. That's all there is to it.

The corpse pose has a variation that I find less comfortable but might be preferable for you. Lie this time on your stomach, legs slightly spread, hands on the floor by your thighs with palms to the sky. Rest your head on one cheek. (This turning of the head to rest on a cheek causes me some strain in the neck muscles, but perhaps I have a tight neck.)

The **folded leaf** is another resting pose. This one is better to use during the course of a Yoga session, while the corpse pose is better at the end, for extended and trancelike relaxation.

Begin by kneeling. Sit back on your heels or even between your heels. Now lean forward, touching your head to the ground or resting it on your knees. Place your arms so that your hands are resting on the floor, palm up, alongside your ankles. Breathe rhythmically and imagine your brain has slipped down into your belly. Eyes closed, imagine you can see it there.

Backward-Bending Poses

An important note: Although I have grouped all the backward-bending poses together here and all the forward-bending poses together in the following section, you should never do only one or the other. A series of backward bends should *always* be followed by a series of forward bends. Ideally, you should alternate each forward-bending pose with a backward-bending pose, or vice versa. If you don't, you will experience the stiffness and pain that comes from imbalance.

The snake is extremely useful for developing ordinarily weak lower-back muscles, for retrieving the original alignment of your spine, and for opening up the breathing passages and cavities. It will stretch out armor in your belly as well as in your throat. When I first did the snake I spontaneously emitted the most delicious of guttural, animal groans. My throat had been so closed up from tension (and my voice, correspondingly, had been so tinny and immature) that this first stretch and release was, for my body, sheer pleasure.

Lie flat on the floor, on your stomach. Now, very slowly, inhaling as you rise, raise your head and chest up off the floor as high as you can without the aid of your hands. Find a comfortable top point—remember, no straining. Breathe in this position as calmly as you can. When you begin to weaken, place your hands on the floor underneath your shoulders and brace yourself with them. Lift up a little higher.

Drop your head back as far as it will go. Stretch out your neck, stretch out your belly. This is the key.

In this completely arched position, begin taking complete breaths. As you retain your breath, arch back *gently* a little farther. *Relax into the pose.* Feel the warmth that it brings as blood circulates through little-used areas of the body. Feel the backward curve of each vertebra in the spine. Focus your mind on your spine. It holds you up. You are many things— among them, a vertebrate.

Now lower yourself *as slowly as you possibly can.* Jerkiness or flopping down can ruin the benefits of your arch and can even be dangerous. Take all the time in the world to lower yourself. As you come to the floor rest your head not on your chin or cheek, but on your forehead. You will feel how this tends to straighten the spine. Press your forehead into the floor, heightening this effect.

Next, adopt one of the relaxing poses (either of the corpse poses or the folded leaf) and breathe normally as you "listen" to your body for the effects of the snake. If at any time during the pose you feel a need to groan or make noises (though not the "oomph" of overstraining effort), go right ahead. As in sex, the groan is your body's way of saying, "I like it!"

If there is any important muscle not stretched by the **total backward pose** it has yet to be discovered. The pose is used not only in Yoga, but as a preliminary warmup exercise in many martial arts (Karate, Aikido, etc.) as well. It has all of the therapeutic effects that have previously been discussed, and it is also a significant aid in banishing tension in the thighs and breathing passages.

The total backward pose is difficult at first for many people, since most of us are rather stiff, so I've included both the half and full versions. When you do this stretch you will find it extremely comfortable and calming, but you'll hurt a bit until you've practiced. The pain is no more and no less than the pain of a body fallow from disuse. (Children can do this exercise the first time with total delight.) Again, though, the admonition not to overstrain yourself must be repeated.

Sit in a kneeling position with your buttocks resting on or between your ankles. Lean backward slowly and place your hands alongside your ankles for support. In the halfway position you may stop at a forty-five-degree angle from the floor. Drop your head all the way back and gaze with wide-open eyes at the ceiling.

For the full total backward pose, slowly drop back even farther, until the back of your skull touches the floor. Tuck your head in so you can see the wall behind you. Your arms may be by your sides, or, for a greater stretch, reaching straight out past your head. Some people like to grab their heels or ankles when doing this pose. Breathe deeply, fully, and slowly as you *relax into the pose*.

When you come up, come up smoothly and slowly. Use your hands and arms for support if you need to, but work toward being able to bring yourself upright without their aid. When you've reached the kneeling position from which you began, do several complete breaths and follow them with several repetitions of the total exhale. Then move slowly and gracefully into the folded leaf resting position.

Work into the total backward pose slowly, and don't be discouraged by initial stiffness. After you've become more supple, you'll find it an easy and powerful way to relax and gain new energy.

The third backward-bending pose is **the boat.** Swami Vishnudevananda says of this pose, "The whole spine is bent like a bow, so this is the best exercise for the cervical, thoracic, lumbar, or sacral region of the spine. The back muscles are well massaged. This removes constipation and cures dyspepsia, rheumatism, and gastrointestinal disorders. It rescues fat, energizes digestion, invigorates appetite, and relieves congestion of the blood in the abdominal viscera. This pose is recommended for women." I'll bet you can't wait to get to it.

Lie flat on your stomach. Raise your chest and head, as if to begin the snake. Now lift your feet and bend your knees. Reach back with both hands and grasp your ankles. Pull the ankles toward you—you will see that as you pull, your trunk and thighs rise up until your only contact with the floor is your stomach.

Hold this pose until you can breathe easily and naturally, without straining. Release your ankles and come down as slowly and gracefully as you can. Relax in the corpse pose.

Now go into the boat pose again. This time, however, you are going to rock the boat. Balance can be frustrating at first, so begin with a very gentle rocking. Only with practice will you be ready for the open sea.

Keeping a tight grasp on your ankles, push backward from your knees. This will raise your torso even higher. Now relax your legs and rock forward (towards your brow). Pull back (and up) with your legs to rock up again. Repeat over and over until you have attained a smoothly flowing rocking rhythm. It's fun to do this to music.

If you have trouble rocking, content yourself with just holding the boat pose. It's enough by itself, really, and as soon as you are able to hold it easily, rocking will come without effort.

Forward-Bending Poses

As a rule, the forward-bending poses are tranquilizing poses. If you think about the little acts of daily life you will see that people instinctively bend forward when they are looking for calm. Rodin's "The Thinker" is a good example.

If you've ever spent a day working in the garden or in a low space where you have to crouch over all the time, you know what sore muscles are and what a sore back is. You get sore from work like this not so much because of the position you're in or the length of time you're in it, but because you *haven't* been in a contrasting position to balance it out. Limbering up the spine as a way of preparing the body for higher consciousness is at the heart of Yoga, and if you bend only one way you will get only soreness and the loss of Yoga's effect for your trouble. Backward bends must always be followed by forward bends (or vice versa). And as you will see when we get into kinetic techniques, a backward bend is almost always the proper moment for an inhale, a forward bend the time for an exhale. (In bending backward, the chest cavity is stretched toward its largest capacity for inhale. In bending forward, it is compressed to its greatest capacity for exhale. Air is literally squeezed from the lungs.) But we jump ahead of stillness. . . .

The **obeisance pose** can be done either standing or

61

sitting. It's thoroughly simple, and because it's simple you should put more effort into experiencing yourself while doing it than into trying to do it "properly."

Standing or seated, grasp your ankles with your hands. If your ankles are "too far away," grasp your lower calves. Lower your head to your knees. Now pull your head closer to your knees by pulling your arms against the ankles (keep your heels on the floor at all times). *Don't* worry about touching your head to your knees—just go as close as you can without strain. Next, achieve a steady, relaxed breathing.

You will find that the steadier your breathing, the more your body will loosen up and the easier it will be for you to approach your knees with your forehead. The ultimate goal of this pose is to do just that —touch your head to your knees—but it may be months before you're loose enough to do it. And, in fact, the point is not to touch your knees with your forehead—the point is to slowly "untie" yourself. Don't be obsessed by the goal, or by how good you are, or even by how much progress you're making. Just do it, and feel yourself. Feel your tight back, your tight stomach, your tight neck, your tight buttocks, your tight thighs, your tight chest. You're really tight, aren't you? Don't worry—everyone is.

A good sign when you're doing the obeisance pose is a tingling or a warmth in the soles of your feet. Sometimes the warmth will spread up your legs and through your body, into your face, as you relax. That's even better. These signs will appear relatively quickly, if you don't strain. They feel really good.

Yogis are proud of **the plough** and rightfully so. It could calm down a madman. If you're experiencing out-of-control anxiety, the plough is the first remedial step you should take. It's an incredibly powerful tranquilizer, and if you do it before going to sleep you'll find you'll never need another sleeping pill. If you're fairly calm to begin with, the plough will take you to that peaceful place so necessary in preparation for meditation.

Lie flat on your back, on, of course, a hard surface. Using your hands to support your buttocks, raise your legs until your feet are over your eyes. Now slowly lower your feet so that your toes gradually come to touch the floor behind your head.

For the best effect your legs should be straight at the knee, but you may be stiff at first, and if you are, some bending is permissible. When you achieve the pose, or something very close to it that's comfortable, begin breathing deeply and regularly. Relax into it. You'll find that it becomes easier and easier the more you relax. In fact, if you relax enough, this seemingly strange and pretzel-like attitude can become as comfortable as an old shoe.

The positive signs in the plough are a relaxed feeling as you attain a steady and controlled breathing, a subsequent easy breathing without control, a warmth and tingling in the soles of the feet—which may spread to the legs and back—and a sensuous, unstrained feeling in the tongue.

The plough can be used to relieve sexual tension even though, for the first few times, it will produce quite a bit of excitement in your genitals.

To do **the dolphin,** lie on your stomach. Lock your hands over your head; your arms make a triangle on the floor. Keeping your knees straight, walk up toward your head on your toes. Keep walking up until you can stand flat-footed on the floor. If you're too stiff at first to do this, let your head come up off the floor and support yourself on your hands. Breathe abdominally, as deeply as possible, as you hold the pose. (To aid in breathing abdominally, you might try pointing your feet in toward each other—that is, standing pigeon-toed.) Try the Breath of Fire in this pose, concentrating on your abdomen as you exhale. Afterward, relax in the corpse pose or the folded leaf.

Head and Shoulder Stands

Head and shoulder stands can be very beneficial, especially since they help the heart to relax and irrigate the brain with blood, but most of these poses are too dangerous for the beginner (who in any event needs individual instruction). Ask any chiropractor— he gets a lot of business from awkward and ignorant first-time headstanders. See your local Yogi.

There is one pose, though, that isn't dangerous and that sends blood to the brain as forcefully as a head-stand—it's

The Crow

Squat. Place your hands on the floor in front of your knees. Slowly tip yourself over toward your hands, inching up to them by walking in tiny steps. Raise your feet off the ground, then your legs. Keep your legs folded and brace a knee against each arm. Balance in mid-air parallel to the floor. You'll know you're doing the right thing when you feel a rush of blood into your head or hear it in your ears.

Another technique for getting blood to your head

and rejuvenating those tired old gray cells is to take a nap with your head lower than your feet.

Basic Yoga Principles

There are certain principles that apply to all the Yoga poses, and these should constantly be borne in mind. As you read the following, think—without getting too profound about it—about the possibility that these principles might apply to your whole life, your whole way of being, and not merely to the Yoga postures. In a sense, all life is a series of postures.

Relax
The poses are supposed to help you grow, not torture you.

Move Gracefully and Slowly
Your body will appreciate this, as a dog appreciates its biscuit.

Don't Strain Yourself
Ask yourself this question: "Can I do more than I can do?" Of course not. Why even try? Ironically, you can make faster progress with less ambition.

Always Rest After a Pose, or After a Series of Two or Three
Yoga is not designed as a system of exhaustion. It's a measured and subtle way of encouraging growth, and the rest periods are when you grow. Without them, you lose all of the beneficial effects.

**Always Alternate Between a Forward Bend
and a Backward Bend**

The two types deal with different aspects of the body, complement each other, and need each other for balance. This is the classic principle of the unity of opposites. If you want a unity, you need to include the opposites. And, in more practical terms, if you don't alternate, you'll get sore.

Relax into a Pose

Feel how the pose feels. Explore your body in its new position. Try to see what you've been missing. To learn something new about your body is to expand your consciousness. To *relax* is to expand your consciousness. Breathe as deeply and as rhythmically as you can.

The purpose of Yoga is to loosen you up—not just while you're doing it, but for all the time. It changes your normal state. The tension of living in civilized life makes you tight, and if you do nothing about it, you get tighter and tighter until you get "old." You can be advanced in years—you can be eighty—without having to become "old." Rigidity is your fate in this society, but your fate is not absolute. Your fate can be in your hands, if you exercise them.

Practicing Yoga

Always begin your Yoga practice with ten minutes of complete breathing and coming to attention.

Never practice Yoga on a bed.

Finish a session with alternate nostril breathing, the total exhale, and the Yogic cleansing breath. Then meditate. (See the chapter on meditation.)

Frozen Movement and Psychological Postures

The Oriental disciplines have certainly proven themselves over time as means to relaxation, better energy, and higher, happier consciousness. But there's something missing in the ways of the East for us in style of being and living. Eastern methods were developed in cultures that had little or no feeling for individuality or even individual worth. On the one hand, this permitted people practicing them to concentrate on "spirituality" and ego loss, which is important; but at the same time, they missed the crucial relationship of the techniques *to the individual practicing them.* Here we probably have the reason that the paths of the East traditionally require a lifetime of work: they aren't geared to the individual. The practitioner must adjust him- or herself to the techniques, because there's little or no room for variation according to individual needs.

Each of us has resistances and blind spots when it comes to seeing ourselves as we really are—Western psychotherapy has known this from the beginning. Part and parcel of our limiting neuroses is their quality of self-maintenance. We are in ruts—ruts that we call self, or personality, or character—and to get *out* of our ruts we need to experience ourselves in all our (glorious) ruttedness. Meditation alone, for example, can do no good unless we knew why it is that we are so uncontrolled and compulsive, why it is that we have such trouble meditating. What good does it do to stretch and loosen our armor if we don't become aware of the mechanisms and habits that tend to tighten us up again?

We are energy systems, but it's not enough to generate energy. We need to know the system like the palms of our hands. Each of us is different; each of us has his or her own special methods of self-limitation, of energy dispersal, of self-destruction. To become aware of ourselves as systems of this type requires more than the mechanical practicing of special "calisthenics." It requires self-analysis, a slow and deliberate contemplation of your feelings—your feelings as they are in your mind, your feelings as they are in your body. Talking helps, as the psychoanalytic experience has shown. But observation is equally important, and there are things you can observe about yourself that you will never get to by merely talking or "thinking on it."

Television and major-league sports, ironically, have proved to us that even in the tangible, material world there is much that we don't see. Life is quicker than the eye. We think a base runner is clearly safe. Looking at the stop-action replay, we can see we were wrong—the ball arrived before the runner did. We were *wrong*. What we thought we saw we didn't see. *We saw something that didn't happen!*

That's why we need the tool of stop-action for self-analysis. We are fully capable of *not* seeing what exists, or of seeing things that don't exist. We're rather fallible as information processors, but by slowing down, by stopping the action altogether, we can become much better.

And until we correctly receive the information that is *ourselves,* our very mode of being, we can't make the kind of progress in self-development that is really possible. All our gains will be wiped out by the retrenching action inherent in our resistance to change.

How to Use the Stop-Action Concept

Everyone has conventionalized, habitual postures and gestures. There are also many postures and gestures that are conventions of social life; they are as habitual as personal manifestations, and equally imprisoning and uncreative. (Some of these, of course, are handy and time-saving, but many are tools of control that keep us in our places—places we're trying to move beyond!) What we're going to do now is to examine some of our "ruts" and see how they affect us—as members of our society and as individuals. We'll see what feelings they create, what feelings they represent, what feelings they *prevent*. Feeling is all-important. Suzanne Langer called the human mind a "feeling intellect." To be complete, you need to *feel* what's happening as well as think about it.

The Name Game

In a sense, this sort of exercise introduces you to yourself in a way you've never been introduced before. When you meet someone, of course, you usually tell him or her your name. . . .

1. Say your name. Say it out loud or silently, but go through all the motions of introduction and move your lips (at least) as you do it. Introduce yourself to yourself. Introduce yourself to your parents. Introduce yourself to a stranger.

2. Now, take the one introduction of these three that brings out the most feeling (really act it out!), and imagine that situation. *Visualize* the person you are introducing yourself to. Say, "My name is [name]," and *stop*. Feel the feelings that are aroused. Feel what has happened to your facial muscles, what

has happened to your lips, your chest, your shoulders, your legs and feet. Freeze in that position. Examine it. Examine yourself. What is your basic posture in relation to *the other,* the person you are introducing yourself to? (That person symbolizes the outer world for you.)

Are you begging for acceptance? Are you threatening? Are you looking for a compliment? Are you pushing away? Are you frightened? Are you confident?

Whatever you are, it's expressed in your face and in your body. Examine that expression—not in a mirror, but from *within,* from the standpoint of your physical feelings. What do you see with your inner eye? Remember, what you see is who you are!

Try saying, "My name is," and then *stop.* Don't say your name—stop just before it. Freeze the posture, freeze the gestures, freeze the face and feelings.

Are you proud of yourself? Do you like your name? Do you feel impotent? Ridiculous? Whole? Fragmented?

Many people tend to forget their names when they stop short of saying them like that. *Your name, like your identity (or lack of it), is a habit.* If you don't say your name right away, in the habitual manner, it fades right into space.

Now go ahead and say the first name that comes into your mind. What is it? What does it mean to you? Is it who you want to be, or someone you're afraid of being?

Feel what happens to your body when you call yourself by a name other than your own. Is it a wish feeling or a fear feeling?

Try introducing yourself by your father's name.

"My name is [father's name]." Act as if you were your father saying it. And *freeze*.

Do the same with your mother's name; act her habits as you call yourself by her name.

How do these two "introductions" relate to your introduction of yourself? What are the similarities, the mimetic aspects, in terms of the pose of your face and body? Which one of them has the greatest influence on you?

Now, in front of a mirror, repeat any of the parts of the exercise that had meaning for you. Notice how the feelings (the physical feelings—the shape of your lips, your eyebrows, your forehead, your eyes) change when you see what you look like. What you see in the mirror is *not* necessarily who you are. It's more than likely who you *want* to be, but you're not the image in the mirror. You're the being behind the face that looks into it, the being inside the body that faces it, and only *you* know what that feels like.

The person that you observe, that you "see," when you stop time with a "freeze" is *you*. It is you in your basic attitude, your basic posture toward yourself and the world. Write down what you've experienced and felt, and your opinions, because you're going to want to forget it.

Include in your note to yourself a careful answer to the following question: "What effect were you trying to create with your introduction, and why?"

Now that you have the hang of it, freeze into the following poses. Feel what they feel like physically, feel how they affect you emotionally. Feel how you change as you change your "act."

1. **Strike a seductive pose** (e.g., looking over your

shoulder at the imaginary seducee). Why should such a pose be effective for seducing another person? Do you have some kind of a secret you might give?

2. **Get down on your hands and knees and beg forgiveness.** Put on your most pathetic, contrite, helpless face. You are worthless, of course; you need help. Try looking at this one in the mirror. What memories does adopting this pose (and all the others) bring up?

3. **Smile.** Do you ever smile for some reason other than because you're happy? Hold your smile and think about all the situations in which you smile when you, uh, shall we say, don't really mean it. How do you *use* your smile to create an effect? How do others use theirs on you?

4. **Stick your tongue out at the teacher.** This should make you feel good—you don't like other people having power over you, but you're afraid to stand up for yourself. Instead, you stick your tongue out as a substitute.

5. **Put your hand over your mouth.** Many of us do this all the time, unconsciously. Freeze like this. Feel how you're holding yourself in. Now, quickly take your hand away and say the first word you think of. Write it down. Write down how you felt about saying it and why you think you held it in.

6. **Stand with your arms folded.** Do you feel more secure when you hold yourself?

7. **Raise your fist as if you were the world's champion.** The world's champion of what? How important is the championship, really? Feel the tightness in your shoulder and triceps when you hold your arm this way.

8. **Frown and shake your finger** as if admonishing someone to behave properly. Who do you imagine

yourself to be shaking your finger at? What's wrong with his or her behavior? Now call yourself by name and frown and shake your finger at yourself. What don't you like about yourself? What have you been doing wrong? *Think* about all the things you've been doing wrong. Are they really so terrible?

9. **Run your fingers through your hair,** and at the end of the stroke, curve your palm so it faces an imaginary person whom you like. The imaginary person is near or is talking to you. Send out a ray from your palm. Freeze, with the ray going out. Anthropologists call this "palming." It's a gesture of flirtation and just goes to show how unconscious the expansion of the body—*your* body, *you*—can be. Check it out the next time you're around a group of people (or on the street), especially in a mixed group. People will be palming like crazy, totally unaware of what their bodies are doing. (They'll also point a foot at the object of their desire, or touch their throats or their noses. Each gesture "speaks" of a different kind of person—e.g., a throat-toucher feels guilty about his or her desire.)

Our bodies are constantly expressing our inner selves—it's called "body language"—and if you *stop,* and examine yourself through that stopping, you'll have a chance to see who you really are. Without that knowledge, there is no way to know *how* to change or *what* to change. And development is always personal, it is always *your* development, not the attainment of some abstract and unknowable Nirvana. It is the clarity within your own eccentric self that's the goal.

This brings us to the more difficult but more rewarding phase of stop-action work. This is the focusing of attention on your specific tensions and armor, the examination and analysis of your particular body-self. This you can only do on your own. You've got to consider yourself, consider what is habitual and characteristic of you, freeze it, and study it. When you've studied it "under the microscope," as it were, you'll soon be able to catch yourself in your daily life and see how your whole system works—in both its productive and its limiting aspects. This self-analysis is the necessary precedent to self-therapy, which is the necessary precedent to really getting high.

Let's say, for example, that you tend to touch your head when you talk. Many people unconsciously touch their temples, or nose, or mouth, or pull their ears. If this is you, apply stop-action to it. Try to isolate the feeling you have when you touch yourself as you freeze in that position. Try to discover what feeling brought about the touching. What memories does the touching give you? What anxieties does it assuage?

Now, very slowly, peel your hand away from your head. You're naked now, in a manner of speaking. You don't really need your hand. The next time you feel it inching up there, just sit on it! It's a shield that you don't need, a habit acquired in an earlier time that only reinforces, now, *today,* armor created in a yesterday.

All such habits must be dealt with similarly. The many techniques in this book can't help you as they should if you have habits that are the henchmen of your restricting armor.

(One way to deal with your body's habits is to exaggerate them so much that they become humorous. If you tend to bend forward from the neck, for example, do a stop-action on it and then do *another* stop-action as you totally exaggerate the position, bending way over like a ninety-year-old man. Exaggerating makes these weaknesses less personal and threatening, and shows you what you're doing to your body by doing *even more* of it.)

The whole idea of stop-action is to locate your armor, and then to try to make the connection between your body and your psyche by locating tension and irregularities. You make a connection between body and mind by studying the *feelings* that you have when you become aware of an energy blockage—armor—and when you do things that, temporarily, at least, remove it.

So go ahead and "act out." You need to feel free and uninhibited about copying your typical physical and emotional attitudes. What you see really *is* what you are, and it's what others see—whether they are consciously aware of it or not.

Interpretive Stop-Action Mime

Taking the concept of stop-action one step further, you will find that there are aspects of your personality that are well hidden physically—they're either repressed or disguised. But you can experience the tensions involved by imitating the conventional poses that are associated with certain emotions. When an actor plays a role well, imitating utterly convincingly the gestures and speech of his character, he does so because he has been able to *feel* the character from the inside. Most of us are better actors than we know, and we each have at least one character that we can play literally to the hilt—ourselves.

It works two ways. First, you can take an aspect of your personality that is dominant and "act" it. Let's say you're passive. You want others to do things for you. Pantomime the role (in private, of course, for now—you want absolutely no inhibiting factors around) of a beggar. Do it as well as you possibly can. Really beg. Tell your benefactor you'll die without his or her help. Then, when you've reached a pitch of passion, you can freeze. Feel your feelings. Feel your body in its pleading pose—one you would never adopt in real life because it has been *shamed* out of you. Just feel it, and feel what it means to you. But *don't* judge yourself—don't say to yourself, This is good or This is bad. Do, though, if you can do it without judging, think about the role of passivity in the way you live your life.

Alternatively, you can take a role that you feel is a very small, repressed, even alien aspect of yourself. The passive person might want to portray an extremely aggressive, masterly individual. Go ahead and mime it with all the dramatic effect you can muster. Then freeze. See if this role is really a part of you that you've been repressing, or whether it's just a role that you think you *should* be able to play, or whether it's actually a role that you *do* play in a different costume!

How does your body feel? Is the alien posture, are the alien gestures, difficult for you to adopt—stressful—or are they easy? This should tell you something about yourself.

The stop-action techniques of still life are all directed toward self-analysis. The mere practice of disciplines of evolution is important, and certainly it has an improving effect all by itself. But if you want to get the most out of changing your body-mind, you must also deal with the self, *your* self, that is doing the exercise. Many people have sought to get *outside* themselves for an escape from themselves, and there are many partial escapes. You really *can* escape, you really *can* become new; but you must look inward as well as outward. Think of yourself in a kind of jail. Before you make your big break, wouldn't you like to know where the guards are posted?

Still-Life Poses for Energy

Although we all readily recognize that we have high periods and low periods, many of us are still skeptical about the concept of inner energy. I have often experienced this myself. Even as nothing could be clearer than that our highs and lows are functions of energy, we feel there must be some trick to it, some illusion. It's probably because inner energy is so much more subtle than other forms—it's almost unmeasurable objectively. It can't even supply enough juice to power the smallest lightbulb.

In the martial art of Aikido they've devised a demonstration to show beginning students the nature of inner energy, which they call Ki.

It's called "the unbendable arm," and while its effect really can't be so great without a teacher present, you can do this on your own sufficiently well to experience a real and tangible energy. I'll explain how shortly.

In Aikido, the martial art most closely allied with Zen Buddhism, it is taught that mind power is far more important than physical strength in combat, and, indeed, in all phases of life. Aikido and Zen practi-

77

tioners believe that the key to being able to use your mind power—they often call it breath power or breath energy—is to develop a focus on the gravitational center point of your body. This center point, they say, is located about two inches below the navel (thus the old and very misguided joke about "contemplating your navel"—in fact, it's an excellent thing to do!) and is called the Hara center.

I have seen Aikido masters perform minor miracles —a man of sixty once knelt on the floor, sending his Ki downward, and he couldn't be budged by five strong young martial-arts students! Though it may seem strange from our Western viewpoint, it is difficult to see how so many masters of Aikido, Zen, and T'ai Chi could be wrong about the location of our physical center. Their physical abilities confirm that they have a very special knowledge.

The power that comes through the body is not muscular, it is mental. And it is unleashed through focusing on the Hara center, through feeling it and encouraging it by will and sending it outward. Will is definitely required; you can't simply remain passive and flaccid, for your energy will not come to you and sweep you away unless you make it happen. Will, yes —but straining, never.

The Unbendable Arm

To do the unbendable arm you need a partner.

1. Kneel in front of your partner with your knees about two "fists" apart; ask your partner to kneel in the same way. There should be about two "fists" of space between you.

2. Now place your arm on your partner's shoulder. Have your partner reach up with both hands and try to bend your arm at the elbow. Feel how you resist

the bending. Feel how you move your weight, and feel especially how the muscles in your arm *vibrate* as you resist. This vibration is muscle power. But we are looking for something different, a different kind of strength.

3. Relax for a minute after your partner has bent your arm (it probably will bend, but even if your partner is weak you will feel the muscles vibrating). Then place your arm on his shoulder once again.

4. This time, spread your hand and point your fingers straight out behind him. Look at him directly, but at the same time try to be looking behind him or through him—don't focus on the "inside" of his eyes.

5. Now breathe deeply a few times, concentrating on your exhale. Your exhale is the time of your power —this is true in every movement of life. Focus your attention on a spot about two inches below your navel. Imagine that a rushing stream of energy is flowing from that point up your body and through your arm, filling your arm as water fills a fire hose.

6. Do *not* flex your muscles. Let the energy fill your hose. Imagine that the energy flows out your arm through your fingers, extending a thousand miles past your partner.

7. Now let your partner try to bend your arm again. Don't use your muscles, only your energy. As he begins to apply pressure, exhale deeply and slowly. Keep the energy flowing through.

There should a big difference this time. If you've kept your concentration, your partner has been unable to bend your arm. Or if he (or she) is strong and has able to bend it, it has been many times more difficult to do so.

Your arm probably won't be totally unbendable

the first time, but you should experience a distinctly different feeling. Your muscles shouldn't vibrate; you should be able, somehow, to keep your arm fairly rigid without them. Believe it or not, you're able to do it by sending Ki, the life force that animates you!

Now have your partner switch roles with you. You will feel how different his arm, his very flesh feels the second time, how the vibration indicating the use of muscles disappears. To hold the relaxed but Ki-filled arm of an Aikido master is to hold what can only be called pure soft power. Sometimes your hand will drop away in fear of his sheer will and energy, which is never, under any circumstances, aggressive.

Ki, life force, is not reserved for use in combat. To be sending Ki, to be flowing outward, is the essence of vitality and a free intelligence. When you are in love, you send Ki, when you succeed in a competition, it is from sending Ki. When you are at your best your energy is flowing through your system and outward, freely, like a fountain, and those around you cannot help but be positively affected by it.

To be a person with outflowing energy is an act of will. It is a potential that you can develop—and, since it is an act of will, you must make a decision to develop the potential. A lack of decision is, in effect, a decision to be wired up only to yourself, to be a closed circuit.

The nature of Ki is mysterious, but it is clear to all who have experienced it that the higher your level of energy—the more you send—the more vast is the *reservoir* of energy that you have available for your needs. It is an infinitely replenishable resource. The only thing that destroys positive energy is neglect and lack of use.

Other Energy Postures

As in the unbendable arm, a useful way of getting Ki to flow is to imagine it flowing out the fingers. Once you have begun the process, you will soon be able to *feel* the Ki flowing out your hands—or your feet, knees, elbows, armpits, eyes, etc.

The following positions are conducive to generating energy flow. Adopt one of the postures and remain motionless. Recall the metaphor of rushing water filling a firehose, making it rigid from within. Take moderate-sized complete breaths and send out Ki as you exhale. Wide-open eyes will help you attain a smooth flow, and there is no better feeling than to feel that you have energy flowing out through sparkling eyes. Finally, as with Yoga, remain relaxed. Never strain. Energy is very subtle, and the weak awakenings of it cannot be felt unless you're calm and relaxed.

To do **the lion,** get down on your hands and knees. Spread your palms wide on the floor. Raise your head so you're looking straight forward or even upward. Open your eyes as wide as you can. Open your mouth and let your tongue hang all the way out. Inhale and exhale vigorously (and rapidly) through your mouth.

With **claws,** you'll build up your wrists as you send energy. Form your hands into the shape of an animal's claws, and hold them in that position with considerable muscular tension. Now hold your hands in front of you and turn them, from the wrists, in circles going in opposite directions. Exhale and send energy when the claws are facing forward. Be sure to make your circles as wide and full as possible.

In a variation of claws, you squat halfway down,

throw your head back, and reach backward with your claw hands, stretching as far back as you can go. Send energy out your eyes and fingertips with each exhale.

To do the **low power stance,** squat down as far as you can; keep your back straight. Stretch your arms out all the way in front of you, palms facing up. Inhale, and then raise your hands to eye level as you exhale. Develop a rhythm of arms-down inhale and arms-up exhale and try this at varying speeds from excruciatingly slow to chaotically fast.

In the **auto charge,** you grasp the bridge of your nose with thumb and forefinger and exhale deeply. As you exhale, press your thumb and forefinger in and upward, ending your motion pushing inward on the nose and upward on the eye sockets. Also try simply pressing in on the soft part of the bridge of your nose with the hard part of your index finger as you exhale. Use plenty of pressure.

Shooting pistols is a good all-American pose. Stretch your arms in front of you and make each hand look like a gun, with your forefingers as the barrels. Do the Breath of Fire, concentrating on your fingertips.

Chapter Five

Movement

As we proceed from still life to the techniques of movement, we will meet more methods for generating and sending energy. Additionally, we will stretch out and loosen your entire body from head to toe, for to get a good flow of energy, you need to loosen body armor as well as apply your will. You might think of your body as a fully laden sponge soaked not with water but with vitality. If the sponge is frozen, stiff, rigid, the vitality it holds cannot be squeezed out. Through movement, your "sponge" will thaw, loosen up—then you will have ways to relax your repression, your inhibitions, your mind and body. And with the power of your will and your new knowledge of how to nurture and encourage energy, you can squeeze the sponge that never goes dry.

Along the way you'll lose weight, your muscle and skin tone will improve, your senses will come newly alive, and you'll become more radiant. And it sure is a lot more fun than jogging.

There are three main thrusts to the movement techniques. Some exercises focus on only one of these; some incorporate all three. First there is stretching, which opens your body to the flow of energy. Secondly, there are techniques that are primarily involved with armor. This second group will help you to become more sensuous and less inhibited in your body; there is almost an auto-erotic quality to successfully getting in touch with yourself. You've got to abandon the body shame that's so ingrained in our culture. You've got to *experience* yourself—at least during your movement sessions—as if you lived your life in a loincloth. Go a little wild with these techniques. It's not going to harm you. You'll feel things, pleasurable things, you've never felt before.

The third kind of movement is "moving meditation." Many people labor under the misconception that you *must* sit still in order to meditate. This is emphatically not true, though sitting still is, of course, one good way to meditate. The heart of meditation is your mental one-pointedness. You can be one-pointed while you're still—and just as one-pointed while you're moving. It's all a matter of concentration. If you can be involved in your movement on two levels —the level of sensuous experience and the level of the observer of the experience (the "self-rememberer")—you can meditate during a variety of repetitive actions.

There is a rather marvelous irony here, too. You prepare yourself for meditation by developing an intensely mindful sensuality, albeit an inner sensuality, a spiritual one. You develop an energy that is, above all, tactile and tangible. You *magnify* your connection to the world. Yet the essence of the power of a moving meditation like dervish whirling is the way it *cuts you off* from external stimuli.

Actually this is only a paradox in that certain Western habits of thought force such extreme antitheses between the tangible world and the intangible one. We need to remember that there is only one sense, really, called *feeling;* it subsumes the other five. In a moving meditation the object of your feeling, of your senses, is *yourself.* Recall the quotation from William Blake:

> . . . when our senses expand
> we perceive the One.

Your mind *is* your senses, though compounded with reason, it becomes much more. If you practice relaxation and the dissolution of body armor, you can direct your mind within or without, *at will.*

Biological scientists often refer to motility, or the ability to move, as the fundamental distinction between dead things and living things. Those who are *most* motile, most fluid and flexible, are usually those who are most alive. People whose bodies move easily also find it easy to feel their emotions and to be expressive. Some people seem to be "born" or "naturally" motile, but in truth we all are born this way. The recovery of your natural flexibility, the renewal of the use of your limbs, the freeing of the conduits between mind and body, is only the realization of a potential you already contain. And this process of awakening, or reawakening, can change your life dramatically—more than anything else you might do.

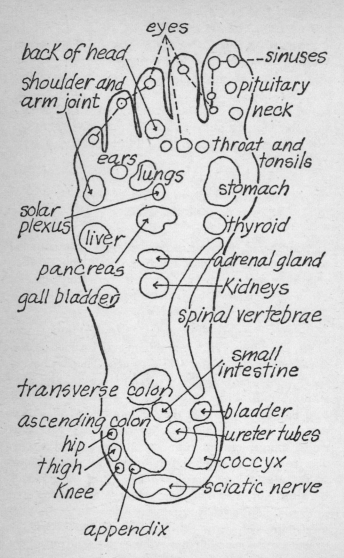

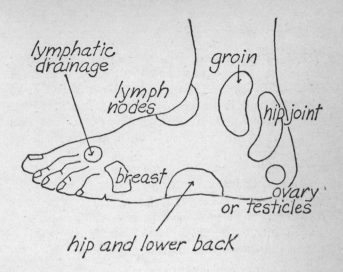

lymphatic drainage

lymph nodes

groin

hip joint

breast

ovary or testicles

hip and lower back

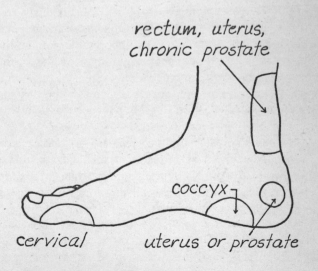

rectum, uterus, chronic prostate

coccyx

cervical

uterus or prostate

Stretching

Now we're going to take a "moving" stretch tour of your body, from toes to scalp. You need to learn about every inch of yourself and how to stretch it so you won't be helpless when you feel some part of your body tensing up from anxiety. We all have our own little ways of getting tense—you'll have to find out exactly what yours are *and* be prepared with the remedy.

None of the following techniques should cause pain, so if you feel any, you'll know that you've come across a spot of particular tension and should work more gently on it. If you work gently and with patience, the tension will inevitably dissolve.

Feet

Most people are unaware of the tremendously important role of their feet in the state of their total energy systems. Nearly every important organ in the body has a nerve connection in the foot (see the illustration). These nerve endings often become congested, and there are specialists, reflexologists and zone therapists, who do *nothing* but foot massage as a form of healing—and it works!

For the majority, though, feet are something you look at sometimes at the end of the bed, or things that get cold (poor circulation!), or things to wrap in shiny leather and abuse all day long by stomping them down on hard cement.

As you become sensitized to your feet, however, you'll see that they're important locations of emotional tension—and one of the easiest means to a happier, more relaxed, more lighthearted state—one foot massage, and you'll be converted.

I keep an old log in my bedroom; it has smooth bark, and it's about six inches in diameter. You should get yourself a log like this. A log is Mother Nature's Reliable and Fully Guaranteed Foot-Therapy Machine.

Place the log in a doorway, so you can brace and balance yourself by holding onto the door frame. Wearing socks, or barefoot, but not wearing shoes, stand on the log with both feet. The log should be pushing up on your arches. Now roll your feet on the log so that pressure is applied in a rolling motion from heel to toe and toe to heel. Keep doing it as long as you can, until all tension is dissolved. (If you have trouble balancing you can do one foot at a time, but be sure all your weight is coming down on that foot.)

When you're finished rolling, lie down in the corpse pose and feel what has happened to your feet. Feel the changes in your head, especially around the temples. Then get up and walk around a little. Feel how relieved your feet and legs have become.

You have a lifetime of tension stored in your soles, as well as congestion built up by any organs that aren't functioning properly. Each day the tension re-forms. Log-rolling is an excellent way to begin your day and to expunge the day's tensions when you come home in the evening.

Toes

After you've worked on the soles, give your toes a massage. Grasp one of your big toes between thumb and forefinger and turn it in wide circles. (This relieves tension in the neck.) Then rub and knead it as if you were making it into a little ball. Do the same to the rest of your toes.

If you feel an identifiable point of pain when you touch the bottom of a foot or a toe, you have located a malfunctioning organ. Spend some time massaging the area. When you have relieved the congestion at the nerve ending the pain will disappear and your organ will begin to function normally again. If the pain persists, consult a physician.

Ankles

Now sit on the floor with both legs stretched out in front of you. Bend one leg and with one hand grasp your leg just above the ankle; with the other, grasp your foot near the ball. Now turn your ankle around and around—try to make the circles wide enough so that you're actually stretching the muscles and ligaments. When you've loosened your ankle up, grasp your leg just above the ankle with both hands, let the ankle go limp, and shake your foot very vigorously as it dangles. Repeat with the other foot.

Calves

Stretching your calves also stretches your feet. Lie flat on your stomach, hands out in front. Now "walk" up toward your head with your feet, thus raising your buttocks and back, until you're resting on your hands and *flat* on your feet, making a camel hump. Hold the position for several seconds. Then return to the prone position by reversing your motion. Repeat.

(You will find that jumping for joy and several of the walks of life to be presented later in this chapter are also excellent calf stretches.)

Knees

Knees are often overlooked, but they can be an extremely sensitive and important part of the body. It's no accident that the classic posture in our society for expressing devotion and intense feelings of gratitude is the kneeling position. Why should this be so? It can't be explained logically, but the knees are an integral part of our body-mind system. Recently, scientists have been able to help deaf people hear by means of electrodes attached to their knees!

Seated, with one leg slightly bent, grasp your kneecap, placing all five fingers around it. Now press down and in as hard as you can, hold the pressure, and relax. Do this several times; then dig down and massage your kneecap with back-and-forth manipulation and circles. With stiff fingers, tap briskly all around the knee. Repeat with your other knee.

Now stand with your legs straight. Bend over slightly and grasp your lower thighs with your hands. Jam your knees together and begin moving them in large circles. Start out slowly, until you can do the motion naturally; then speed up until you're going as fast as you can. Then go even a little faster. Keep your feet planted on the floor. Your knees, of course, must bend as you move around in the orbit.

Next, squat with your feet about eighteen inches apart. Rest your hands on your knees. *Keep your back straight.* Hold this squat as long as you can. Do complete breaths while you're squatting. Afterwards, shake your legs out vigorously.

(Squatting can also be an excellent position for meditating—when you've learned to balance in the pose. Don't forget to keep a straight back! This position happens to be my own personal favorite.)

Finally, make believe there's a soccer ball in front

of you. Kick slowly at it from the knee. Kick it all the way downfield—from the knee, not from the hips, and one leg at a time, of course. Exhale vigorously through your nostrils with each kick.

Thighs and Buttocks

In many people the thighs and buttocks are heavily armored. Often few sensations are really felt there, except on the surface of the skin. It's extremely important to stretch your thighs, especially the ligaments of the groin.

Since slow motions and jumping for joy (later in this chapter) tend to work most of all on thighs and buttocks, we will reserve this space for stretching the groin ligaments. Your thighs and buttocks will stretch simultaneously with work on these ligaments.

The groin ligaments, which connect your thighs to your pelvic area, are taut in most people, and they serve to inhibit fluid movement in your legs—which are your connection to the very ground that supports you. Tight ligaments also force the buttocks together, especially among people in sedentary occupations, cramping and putting unnatural pressure on the anus. This leads to constipation, improper elimination, and the building up of poisons in your body.

When you first begin to stretch these overlooked ligaments you will see how *tight* your body is, and yet how pleasurable it can be to bring it back to its normal elasticity and looseness. Most people in our society walk like wooden soldiers, and this is due almost entirely to taut ligaments and their cohorts, rigid pelvic muscles.

The ability to move and pivot quickly on your legs is important in Aikido; in this martial art the practitioner is always literally running circles around his opponent. To pivot well, with a wide sweep, you have to have stretched ligaments. The two techniques that follow are taken from the Aikido warm-up exercise routine and are also widely used by modern dancers.

For the first exercise, sit cross-legged on the floor. Now move your knees farther to the sides and press the soles of your feet together while resting your feet on the floor. Still keeping your feet on the floor, push down on your right knee with both hands (toward the floor) in a series of quick motions. Then push all the way down in one long, slow action and hold your leg down as you feel the stretch all over your inner thigh.

Do the same with your left knee. Then press down on both knees at the same time.

The harder you press the greater, of course, is the stretch. And you obtain the greatest stretch possible by keeping your heels as close to your body as you can. You can do this exercise in bed, if you like, since you can obtain a stretch simply by pulling your heels close to your groin.

To do **the low-slung buddha,** stand with your legs spread as wide as you can spread them while still comfortably maintaining your balance. Turn your toes completely outward so that your heels are facing each other (as much as possible), and bend halfway down from your knees. Keep your back straight—this is important—and keep your head up, eyes looking straight ahead. Rest your hands on your thighs. You should look something like this:

First practice simply getting into this position—*slowly, very slowly*—and then, just as slowly, rise back up to a straight-kneed stance. When you're able to do it fairly easily it's time to add movement. Main-

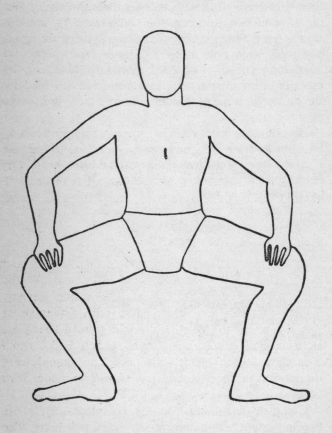

taining a straight back, move in this half-crouch by walking—slowly!

You'll soon see that this is a tremendous leg developer as well as a ligament stretcher and a technique for calming down. Do it in the morning or any time you have an extra minute. The stretching and extra circulation will greatly improve your "groundedness"—your sense of being an animal that walks on the earth—and will help lower your body center to its rightful spot (a few inches below the navel). The concentration on your lower extremities required by this exercise tends to empty your head—hence, its calming function.

The low-slung buddha also works as a rejuvenating sexual stimulant for many people—in fact, techniques that calm you and lower your center often work this way. After all, it's physical tension that is most often responsible for a lowering of sex drive and sexual sensation.

Stomach and Hips

Stomach problems, along with neck ailments and headaches, are the most common (and usually the first) physical manifestations of tension and anxiety. Wilhelm Reich's son remarked that his father never patted him on the head. He would instead touch his stomach and exhort him, "Keep a soft belly, son." You should keep a soft belly, too. You should work the tension out as it comes in, refusing to allow it to become a frozen ice pack.

Complete breathing and the complete exhale are two important techniques for keeping a soft belly. The Kundalini Breath of Fire works well, too, as does the Yogic cleansing breath. The snake and the total forward bend will also help you keep your middle flexible.

In addition to these, try **stomach rolling.** Children often do this for fun, and, like many children's activities, stomach rolling is an instinctive tension releaser. First, tense the top muscles over your stomach, near the solar plexus. Then suck in the middle muscles, and finally the lower muscles near the pubis. (As in the complete breath, the entire motion—all three stages—should be smooth and flowing, so that as you watch your stomach it looks like a rolling sea.) When you've tensed the bottom muscles you can let all three parts relax and then start again from the top. Do it over and over, aiming for a smooth repetitive movement.

Another excellent exercise for stomach and hips is that old Sixties dance, **the twist.** But when you do it, remember that you're not dancing—you're stretching and removing tension from your muscles. How you look as you do it is unimportant. Keep your feet planted on the ground. Swing your whole upper torso, arms and all, *all* the way to one side, then *all* the way back to the other side. Turn your head over your shoulder on the side you're twisting to. Hold for an instant at the farthest point of your twist, and twist a little farther. Imagine that you're wringing water out of your body.

A third, and really the best, way to release stomach tension is to copy your body's natural method, which is vomiting.

Take a few glasses of water and induce vomiting by pushing your finger gently down your throat. Although this is one of the most powerful tension releases known, you should *not* do it if the idea repels you, as it does many people. It's better to get along without it than to generate even more tension by forcing yourself to do something you don't want to do.

Sides

The sides and ribs are hard to work on, but, fortunately, they don't seem to be repositories of a great deal of tension. To stretch them, stand with your hands over your head, fingers reaching to the sky. Reach up as high as you possibly can. Then simply sway all the way over to the left (still keeping arms and fingers outstretched) and back all the way over to the right, in a pendulum motion. (For an extra benefit to the rest of your body, do this up on tiptoes.) When you sway over to the side, your uppermost hand should be approaching waist level. If it doesn't, you've got too much fat blocking your path, so keep at it. You can lose inches from your waist while becoming more flexible, open, and relaxed.

As you work on stomach, hips, and sides, bear in mind that these are the most active areas in the Middle Eastern belly dance, which is known in that area of the world as the "therapy dance."

Chest

Your chest, unfortunately, is a treasure chest of anxiety and emotional armor. Even more distressing is the fact that it is among the most difficult areas to free up. If you look at other people, you will soon see how what a telling repository of personality the chest is. Aggressive men usually have puffed-out rooster-chests—they look a little as if they could push their way through any obstacle with their chests. Retiring, unconfident men often have hollow, inward-curving chests that seem all but collapsed. The same kinds of patterns exist in women, though they are often disguised by unusually large or unusually small breasts—which themselves can be functions of emotional armor. In fact, the suffering of women from chest armor is that much more severe because of the breast fixation in our society.

You may not have noticed it before, but it is often true that when we are feeling our best (when we are in love, for example), there is a warmth and a "rosiness" in the chest that results from a temporary dissolution of the emotional armor. It was noticed by the Persian poet Hafiz in the Middle Ages—he said:

> . . . and the Poet knows Love
> by the Warmth in his Breast . . .

Chest breathing, followed by a total exhale in which the entire chest-and-rib cavity is collapsed and forced inward, is a very useful technique for loosening up a congested chest. And a special method I have developed for this is called **the butterfly and the cocoon.** You may do it seated or standing, but seated is probably most effective—you won't need to worry about balance. It can be done almost anytime, and does not need to be preceded or followed by other techniques.

Holding your back straight, throw your head backward until your skull is touching your spine. Arch backward as you do this. Now spread your arms wide and point them backward, bending your hands back from the wrists as far as you can. As you go backward with head, hands and arms, inhale deeply. Don't overdo the backward motion—go only far enough to feel a stretch, especially in the beginning. As always, don't strain.

Now, in a fast motion, exhale as you bring your head all the way forward (chin to chest). Bring your elbows together in front of you, with your arms parallel and your wrists in front of your forehead.

Repeat this until you're huffing and puffing like a locomotive. The chest is like stew beef—not exactly easy to soften.

Shoulders and Shoulder Blades

The shoulders are another area highly responsive to anxiety. When we feel pain we often hunch our shoulders, and precious few people have shoulders that are customarily relaxed.

One good way to relax your shoulders is simply to think about it. Stand or sit and just let them drop. You'll be surprised at how high you ordinarily hold them. Reich used to talk about generals who wore their medals *under* their chests, and clothes-horses who left the hangers in when they dressed. The abnormal position in which most people hold their shoulders indicates a chronic tension in the related muscles and ligaments. These can be loosened by **hanging.**

Find a convenient branch, jungle gym, or door. Grasp it and hang down with your whole weight. Your feet can even be on the floor as long as you're hanging on untensed arms with all your slowly loosening poundage.

Shoulder rolls will loosen you up, too. Let your arms hang limp. Move your shoulders *only*, keeping your torso straight, in large, slow circles. Pretend you have little bells on top of each shoulder that you are trying to ring.

A third way to stretch your shoulders is to do **the airplane spin.** Here you spread your arms wide and make large circles with them. Try to do this fast, making a breeze, as if you were going to take off.

Also try it while walking—you'll get a rather eerie and pleasant sensation. Your arms should extend behind you far enough to create a little cracking along your upper spine and neck, or in your shoulder blades.

Neck

We will hold off on the neck for the moment, for it deserves, and will get, special attention later in this chapter.

Jaws and Mouth

You might think that this part of your body is less in need of exercise and "undoing" than any other, considering its constant activity. In fact, the truth is quite the contrary. It is here (and in your eyes) that all the defensiveness in your personality—the very defensiveness that blinds you to yourself and cuts you off from your real feelings—finds its most useful ally.

Our use of the oral apparatus is utterly and completely habitual. The way in which we speak, the position our mouth and jaws assume, is our most identifying feature. And, almost by definition, the one identity we *do* have tends to exclude the other identities we *might* have. We stabilize ourselves through our mouths, we give ourselves an oral signature—and we simultaneously stabilize the level of our ability to *feel* ourselves.

Have you tried to keep a "stiff upper lip" or a "tough jaw"? These are ways of repressing feelings of vulnerability or fear, ways of trying to exist *in direct denial of the feelings you actually have*. For the next few days, try looking only at people's mouths when they talk to you. I guarantee that the most guarded, secretive, and rigid individuals—and the most frightened—will *have* that proverbial "stiff upper lip." It will barely move when they speak; it will be taut and uncomfortable-looking when they smile. Sometimes the entire area from lip to nose will appear numb and discolored, whitish. To me, the stiff upper lip is the classic sign of the emotional cripple produced by our society. Most of us have it to some extent.

As Alexander Lowen and Fritz Perls have pointed out, the jaws are our cold-storage warehouse for anger and rage. Think of what clenched teeth mean to you. Think of the jutting jaw of the man who is always ready for a fight. Think of the retracted jaws of the timid, the immobile jaws of the frightened, the jaws of the performer opened to an unnatural extent when he speaks.

Lowen found that when he asked fearful and insecure people to stretch their jaws, they experienced nausea and cold sweats. The mere opening of the mouth let loose a flood of emotional realities stored there. Perls wrote a book called *Hunger and Aggression* in which he showed a direct correlation between how people chewed their food and how much repressed hostility they had.

What is your body's natural method for relieving tension when it is getting ready to sleep (and at other times)? Why, it's the yawn, which stretches out the muscles of the jaw. (I will discuss the importance of yawning at length later in this chapter.)

Nearly all of the following jaw and mouth techniques should be done until they make you feel warm. That's the special peculiarity of this area—when you open it up you get a sensation of warmth. You may also feel a sympathetic vibrating in the back of your neck.

You should be aware that you are entering a rather

sensitive zone. The loosening of emotional armor, particularly around the mouth, will often give rise to negative feelings following that initial rush of energy. You must be strong and self-willed when this happens, and realize that you are not the *feelings*, you are only *experiencing* them. The you that is released from its bondage of armor is the real you, negative feelings are only your defensive personality's way of attempting to regain itself, to ward off change which it fears. Remind yourself that although feelings are your contact with yourself and reality, there is a *you* that feels the feelings, that is *more* than the feelings. It is this *you* who can choose to repeat the exercise, loosening the armor a little bit more each time, working yourself toward spontaneity, freedom, and guiltless high energy.

First do the Kundalini Breath of Fire to raise the level of oxygen in your blood. You're going to need it for areas that have been short of oxygen and nutrients for far too long. Return to normal breathing when you have built up a good tingling sensation and clearness in your head.

Now thrust your lower jaw forward until your lower teeth extend far beyond your upper teeth. Feel the pull and stretch in your jaw below your ears, and gradually stretch your chin even farther forward, until you can stretch it no more. Hold this position. If you feel anger at something or someone, take note of it now. Fantasize yourself in the first situation that comes to mind and take note of that. These are things you have been repressing.

Slowly bring your lower jaw back to its normal position. Rest a minute, then extend it again. Repeat five times at first, and build up your repetitions over time.

When you feel you have really begun to stretch out your jaw, add this variation. From the forward-thrust position slowly move your lower jaw around to the left, so that the right part of the jaw is being stretched sideways. Return to the center, out-thrust position and then move your jaw slowly over to the right. You should move sideways in an arc that is determined by the pull of the rear jaw muscles. Spend some time moving back and forth from side to side, always in a smooth arc and always striving for the greatest possible forward thrust.

This next exercise works on both jaw and lips, and will loosen and bring circulation to your entire face. It creates greater definition of facial features and brings a radiance to your facial skin.

Open your mouth as wide as you possibly can. The opening should not be oval, it should be round—open both vertically and horizontally. Make your face into a gaping mouth. Raise your eyebrows way up on your forehead. With mouth open, take the largest inhale you can, making sure to expand both diaphragm and chest.

Hold your breath for five seconds. Then quickly scrunch up your face into a prune. Force everything toward your lips, which you should extend as far forward as possible in an exaggerated kissing pucker. Simultaneously, exhale forcefully through your nostrils. (The exhale and the closing of the features should begin at the same moment.)

Breathe normally a few times and repeat. Build up your ability to do this exaggerated stretch and ex-aggerated contraction until you can do it very rapidly, omitting the held breath and the pause to return to normal breathing.

After a session of doing this rapidly, relax while gently massaging your face by moving your open palms in small circles.

A variation: When you close your mouth rapidly, crack your front and lower teeth together. The vibration this creates travels directly to your brain and is extremely stimulating.

Your lips require special attention independent of the jaw. One easy way to work on them is through self-massage. Grasp the entire lower lip between thumb and forefinger and pull it outward. Roll it up and down between the fingers as if it were a piece of dough you were trying to shape into a ball. Pull it all the way over to the left, then all the way to the right, then down toward the chin and up toward the nose.

Repeat with the upper lip. Spend twice as much time on the upper lip as the lower lip.

Blowing is also good for your lips and, indeed, the entire mouth, including your cheeks. Puff up your cheeks as if you were playing a tuba. Then blow out through pursed lips, making a raspberry sound. Don't be shy about it—really let 'er rip! For even greater effect, fill your mouth with hot water and blow it out like a whale spout. This is good to do in a bath, and you can do it whenever you go swimimng. Blow over and over, and imagine that you're blowing out tension and stored anxiety each time you do it. You shouldn't have much trouble imagining this, for in fact it is exactly what you're doing. You might even think of someone or something you are trying to "blow out" of yourself.

Here are three more mouth and lip exercises:

Roll both lips inside your mouth, stretching them over upper and lower teeth. Close your mouth. Then release and blow them back out to normal, making a puffing sound.

Make an enormous smile. Then make a tight little O shape with taut lips. Then stretch out again to your smile. Repeat as rapidly as you can, over and over again.

Stick your tongue out—let it see the light of day, let it feel the softness of the air. Breathe vigorously through your mouth. Move your tongue in every direction and contort it into every shape you can think of. Push against your teeth with it. Fold and press it on your palate. Think of the marvelous pleasure it brings you. Think about what a *miracle* it is.

Eyes

Just as most of us suffer the limitation of a characteristic way of speaking, of using our jaws, lips, and tongue, we also tend to have many habitual responses we make with our eyes. Think for a moment, for example, of how *automatic* your eyes' responses are when you're looking at someone or something that bores you.

The eyes are the "mirror of the soul" and they are also, sadly, its curtain. The limited repertoire of your eye movements, your eyes' stiffness and rigidity, are strong reinforcers of your habitual personality patterns. Your eyes drain you of energy when they're not motile, too, for a great deal of energy is used in creating the unconsciously "blocking" stance.

We all know how hard it is to trust a person with nervous, jerky eyes, and how domineering someone with a fixed, authoritative gaze can be. We experience in the eyes of others not only the souls of the others, but equally the lack of soul. You can help let your soul realize itself by giving it a pair of eyes that do not forever hold it in an inescapable prison.

Bring energy to your eyes the way you do when you experience your strongest emotions—love, hate, fear, surprise, awe. When you're really moved, awake, and alert, your pupils dilate and your eyes **open wide.**

So open them wide now, and feel the energy usually reserved only for powerful emotional experiences rushing to them. Open them wide enough so that you can feel cool air under your eyelids. Think slowly of beauty, love, hatred, fear, anger, wonderment, disbelief. Then think only that you are seeing the most beautiful man or woman in the world (depending on which you'd rather see). Try to relax with your eyes wide open, breathing deeply through your nostrils. When your vision starts to blur, close your eyes and rest them. Then do it all over again. (While resting, masage your eyes gently with your fingertips to improve blood circulation.)

The Yogis, Reichians, and bioenergeticians each have a series of techniques (all similar) to relax the tense muscles of your eyes. Although the idea may seem foreign to you, it's important to approach eye exercises with the attitude that your eyes are stiff and rigid, held in place by emotional armor. You will realize that this is indeed the case as you see that the

techniques are difficult and awkward at first, but that
as you practice, your eyes develop an elasticity that
you had previously never imagined possible.

To do the **eye stretch,** begin with your eyelids closed
and roll your eyes around, as children do, very lightly
—five or six rolls to the right, then five or six to the
left. (As with bending in Yoga, whenever we work
on the eyes in one way we must maintain a balance
by doing the same thing on the opposite side or in the
opposite direction.)

Relax a few moments; then open your eyes. Keeping your head straight, gaze in front of you. Then
raise your eyes vertically, still keeping your head
straight, so that you can see the tops of your eye
sockets and the ceiling. Hold that position for a
moment, experiencing the stretching of muscles and
the rarely felt sensations at the top of the eye sockets.

Then drop your eyes straight down so that you can
see the bottom of your eye sockets and your cheeks.
Use just a little extra effort to get them down as far
as possible—this should be done for *all* eye positions.
The idea is to use your eye muscles *more* than you
ordinarily do. Again, focus your attention on the
stretched muscles and the new sensations you're experiencing.

Return your eyes to a normal position and take a
few complete breaths.

Next, look sidelong all the way to the left. Your
left eyeball should be completely to the outside of the
left eye socket, your right eyeball should be thrust
over right against the base of your nose. Hold to the
left for a while, then look all the way over to the
right.

Return your eyes to a normal position and take a
few complete breaths. Rub your palms together until

they are warm and press the warmth into each eye (with the eyelids closed). Remember that, as in Yoga, the proper procedure is exercise liberally interspersed with rest—not activity unto exhaustion.

Now imagine your field of vision to be the 360 degrees or twelve hours of a clock. (When you looked straight up it was twelve; down was six, to the left was nine, to the right was three o'clock.) This time look up to a point between ten and eleven o'clock. Hold that position, concentrating, as before, on what you're feeling. Then look down to a point between four and five o'clock. Proceed to a point between one and two o'clock, and then over and down to between seven and eight o'clock.

Return your eyes to a normal position. Take complete breaths. Rub your palms together and cover your closed eyelids with the warmth.

Repeat this—looking in all eight directions—a total of five times. Remember to rest and apply warmth at the indicated intervals.

When you are able to move your eyes in all eight directions easily, it is time to combine your movements into the **contiguous eye stretch.** This exercise is basic to Yoga and a primary technique in Reichian and bioenergetic techniques, in which it is combined with a dissolution of chest armor.

The **Yogic method** of doing the **contiguous eye stretch** is as follows: Sit or stand upright with your back straight but not rigid. Putting your chin out slightly, look straight ahead. Raise your eyes to twelve o'clock—but raise them only as high as you can *without* straining. Now move your eyes slowly around the boundaries of your eye sockets to the right. Keep the eyes extended to their outermost point continuously. Go all the way to three o'clock, then continue around the bottom of your eye sockets toward nine o'clock and up and back to twelve o'clock. Close your eyes and apply heat generated by rubbing your palms together.

During the entire circle, which should be done *slowly* for best results, remember to keep your eyes stretched out to the farthest possible point. When you find a spot where your eyes want to "skip," return to it and go over the area carefully, working out the tension. These "skip" spots are the locations of emotional armor, and if any thoughts come to you when you hit one it would be wise to write them down.

Follow these instructions carefully, starting out with seven minutes of eye stretching and resting, then building up your endurance and your smoothness. You can do eye stretching anywhere, and there's no need to do it in combination with other techniques. Soon you'll notice that when you're depressed or anxious your eyes feel particularly tight and "locked." By doing the eye stretches at times when you can really *feel* the relationship of body to emotional state, you will relieve yourself, strengthen yourself for the future, and save countless unnecessary hours of misery.

The **bioenergetic** or **Reichian variation** on **contiguous eye stretching** has all the advantages of the Yogic method, and adds the release of chest armor. As you practice this variation you will experience a sharp heightening of energy and a clarity in your head. It takes a little extra coordination, but if you're patient and learn to do it you'll be amply rewarded.

Lie down on a bed or the floor—be sure you're lying flat. Begin inhaling through your nostrils into your chest. Expand your chest as much as you can. Exhale through your *mouth*. As you exhale, let yourself moan your most basso "ahhhh." Force all the air out of your chest, collapsing the lungs and rib cage—really squeeze it out. (You can even have a friend help you by pressing down on your chest as you exhale.) Keep moaning "ahhhh" throughout your exhale, down to the very end.

Build up a rhythm that suits you. Then begin to apply the Yogic method of contiguous eye stretching. Traverse the widest possible circle with your stretching eyeballs. When you "skip" a spot, go back to it and gently work over the area until it goes more smoothly. Keep breathing and moaning, as described above, throughout.

Your breathing may "want" to change as you do this, getting faster or slower or deeper or shallower. Let it just follow along. But remember to continue moaning and saying "ahhh" and rotating your eyeballs. If you feel like moving your body or stretching your limbs while you're doing this that's okay too—in fact, that's a very good sign.

Do the bioenergetic variation until you get tired. Then do *just a little more*. This slight extra push will help you get past resistances and help insure the free flow of the energy you have generated. Rest in the corpse pose after applying heat to your eyelids with your palms.

This technique brings up so much energy that energy literally bounces around in your body, bounces against the energy blockages within. After doing this exercise you will often feel a spontaneous desire to loosen up other areas. Don't ignore this yearning. Seize the time. Following through on the body's own desire for liberation and change is the surest path to permanently raising your level of energy—and your consciousness.

Brow

In earlier times, it was fashionable among poets to refer to the quality of a person by describing that person's brow. We will retain the terms low-, middle- and high-brow. Though the brow is no longer an important part of our vocabulary of knowing people, the poets must have had *something* in mind. Perhaps you can figure out what it was by thinking of the brows (eyebrows to hairline) of all the people you know. You will probably conclude that an open and honest person usually has a mobile and elastic brow, while a rigid person usually has one that looks something like the front of a football helmet.

Here are three exercises for your brow:

Raise your eyebrows all the way up, as if you were guilty but pretending to be innocent. Then scrunch them down in the deepest frown you can make. Raise them again and repeat over and over until you can do it no more. If you're able, try doing it first one side, then on the other.

Place your hands on your forehead with the fingers touching—press in so that the fingertips make a line right down the middle of your forehead. Press hard. Then draw both hands, still pressing hard, across the forehead to each ear. Continue until you feel a slight buzzing sensation.

Massage your forehead all over in small circles, applying strong pressure with your fingertips.

Scalp

Massage every inch of your scalp vigorously. To stimulate circulation even more, grab clumps of your hair and give sharp tugs. With straight fingers, tap on the crown of your skull as if knocking for admittance. Then continue to tap all over your whole skull. Grab your ears and move them in circles. Pull on your lobes. Get some blood in there!

Neckwork

As I mentioned before, your neck is special and deserves special attention.

Most physicians and psychiatrists at this point in history agree that your neck is the first part of your body to show symptoms of anxiety. Headache researchers have found that the vast majority of headaches are caused by constriction—tension—in the neck muscles. When your neck becomes tense it restricts the flow of blood to your brain. And a headache, far from being a mere annoyance, is a serious warning being given you by your body. The warning is: *Stop*. Whatever you're doing that causes the headache—and this you must discover for yourself—you must *stop* doing. Try to become aware of your neck. If you do, and if you take remedial action for neck tension right away, you may never have a headache again.

Psychologists, too, have recognized the importance of neck tension. When we say, "It gives me a pain in the neck," we're doing more than using a figure of speech. It is a literal reflection of the tension we feel, even though we may be completely unaware of the tension on a conscious level.

Neck tension, when severe or chronic, has been shown to cause impairment of vision and of the olfactory sense. Chronic tension can cause a person to hold his or her head in an unnatural position to try to alleviate the tension. This unnatural position means that the spine will be bent improperly and that the internal organs will have an unnatural degree of pressure put upon them. Such pressure weakens the organs, makes them susceptible to disease and functional disorders.

Your neck is the connection between your head and your body. Presumably, you are trying to integrate the two. How can the energy you develop through relaxation and somatic techniques flow to your brain if a constricted neck is damming up its only passageway?

Every investigator of consciousness development has sooner or later come to understand the importance of the neck. Numerous exercises have been developed to un-knot it and relax it—and to keep it unknotted and relaxed. Here are some of the best. Remember—as in Yoga, you must be extremely careful not to overstrain yourself.

Throat Stretch

When we get anxious, we tend to "choke up." Our voices lose their depth and resonance; we find it hard to speak or eat or breathe. This "choking up" is, again, more than a figure of speech. It's a literal description of a somato-psychic phenomenon. Since our customary state is far from relaxed, we are, in a sense, always choking—choking on our part in life, choking on the people around us, choking on our own images of ourselves and how we feel about ourselves.

The throat stretch is quite simple, but it works. Sit

113

in a chair with your back straight (even slightly rigid) with your spine "locked." Now gently drop your head backward *all the way*. Your skull should rest on the top of your spine or thereabouts. If you need to arch backwards to do this or find it more comfortable, that's okay. Hold this position, and keep your attention on your throat. Breathe light and shallow at first; then build up to deeper breathing *as your body dictates*. Don't try to force a deeper breath—simply tune in to yourself and breathe more deeply when you're ready for it. Ordinarily, deeper breathing will occur spontaneously as you allow yourself to relax.

After two or three minutes, raise your head as slowly and gently as you can. Then—slowly, always in control—drop your head forward until your chin is touching your chest. Hold that position for a length of time equal to that for which you dropped backwards. Don't concern yourself about your breathing in the forward position—just let whatever happens happen. Do be sure that your chin is on your chest, however, and that you're stretching the muscles of your neck in a gentle manner. There should be pressure, but no straining or vibration of the muscles. Try to feel the muscles, and be sure that you're stretching the entire muscle length, from base of neck to about halfway up the back of your head.

Isometrics

Isometrics are useful for the neck and should be done as part of your neckwork, but they should be done along with other exercises and not overdone— they can cause stiffness if you're not careful.

Clasp your hands and place them on your head at a point midway between the crown of the skull and the hairline. Pull down on your head as if you were going to push it inside your chest. Resist this movement by flexing your neck.

Next, clasp your hands behind your head and pull forward. Again, resist the pulling with the power in your neck, so a stasis is achieved.

Do the same on each side of your head. You can also do these isometrics by pressing the four sides of your head against a wall, if you prefer.

"Oh Yes" and "Oh No"

These techniques are excellent for loosening your neck and can also yield a great deal of information about your psychology. Pay particular attention to the feelings that arise when you are "yes-ing" and "no-ing."

Do these exercises in some place that's private so you won't feel in any way inhibited. These are exercises you've really got to get into, really got to let go in—otherwise they won't have the proper physical effect and won't release feelings that you may have been repressing but that you will want to know about.

Sit or stand in a relaxed posture. Begin nodding your head to indicate "yes." Do it just as you would if you were ordinarily signifying agreement or assent. Gradually allow your up-and-down swing to increase. You should feel a slight stretch of your throat on the backswing and a pulling of the muscles on the back of your neck as you go downward. Now, as you "yes" in this somewhat exaggerated manner, silently mouth the words "oh yes"—"oh" on the backswing, "yes" on the downswing. Mouth the words with great exaggeration, so that your lips and cheeks are vigorously stretched.

Now pretend there's someone in front of you to whom you are saying "oh yes." It could be anyone—

friend, lover, parent, enemy, boss—but be sure it is a *specific* individual. The first person who comes to mind will probably work best for you.

How do you feel? Docile? Hostile? Friendly? Defensive? These are the secret feelings that are *always* operating on an unconscious level during your interactions with others. This is who you are, though not necessarily who you have to be. Attitudes toward others and toward yourself are malleable—you can change them—but you first must recognize them as your own.

Imagine "yes-ing" other people. What are your secret attitudes in a variety of situations, with a variety of people?

As you do this exercise, let yourself go increasingly. Become *involved* with the "yes" motion, mouthing "oh yes" in a variety of exaggerated ways, and notice the hidden attitudes that are revealed by the procedure. Make your motions longer and more vigorous, stretch your mouth as far as it can go when you say the syllables. Allow yourself to speed up until you experience strong and violent emotions. Stay with it. Loosen up the stored anxiety in your neck and learn its contents. There are great discoveries to be made here, so try to be aware of everything that is happening to you. Don't concern yourself with whether you're doing it "right." Just do your best and focus on all that you are experiencing.

Slow down gradually, as if you were a pendulum running out of momentum. Lie down and rest your head, or rest it on a table. Take several deep complete breaths.

"Oh no" is the counterbalancing technique in this series. Do it the same as "oh yes," but shake your head to indicate disagreement or refusal and say "oh no." Focus on the feelings and attitudes that arise, and remember them. Exaggerate the mouthing of the words. Try jutting out your lower jaw as you do it.

One important difference for "oh no"—don't let yourself get going too fast. If you do, "oh no" can cause dizziness and nausea.

When you've done both "oh yes" and "oh no" to your own satisfaction, try varying the procedure by alternating one complete "oh yes" and one complete "oh no." You'll be making a kind of cross with your head and neck.

Neck Rolls

Neck rolling is an important exercise used by Yogis, martial artists, Sufis, dancers, Reichians—nearly everyone concerned with relaxation and development of high energy.

Neck rolls are simple to do, perhaps deceptively so, and are quite similar to the contiguous eye stretch.

Sit or stand with your back straight. (If you stand, keep your hands on your hips.) Allow your head to drop down on a flaccid neck until your chin touches your chest. Begin an inhale, and as you do so, turn your head to one side and roll it up your shoulder and around until it is in the full dropped-back position. At this point you should have completed your inhale. Now begin to exhale and roll your head back down the other shoulder until you're back at the starting position. Rest and repeat.

Do the complete cycle of the neck roll over and over again until you can actually feel the relaxing effect. Always be sure that your head is stretched as far to the outer boundaries of its circle as the neck will allow it to go. Don't be alarmed if you hear a bit of snap, crackle, and pop when you do neck rolling. That's perfectly natural and will subside as you become more flexible and relaxed.

You may go as slow or as fast as you like, but a period of neck rolling in one direction must be followed immediately by a period of equal duration going in the *opposite* direction.

Roll your neck whenever you feel tense or fatigued. If you do it in the morning, your day will be completely different. Neck rolling followed by the contiguous eye stretch is an ideal combination for making you feel calm, alert, and clear-headed.

The Middle Eastern Nod

The nod is not something done by the users of hashish—it is actually a movement that occurs in belly dancing (also called "therapy dance"), folk dance, and Sufi rituals. The nod has a particularly good effect on the thalamus gland, which means it brings you both relaxation and smooth energy in a single technique.

Sit cross-legged on the floor, or, if you are unable to do this, sit on the edge of a hard chair. Rest your hands on your thighs just above the knee.

Focus your attention on your chin—although this is basically a neck exercise, the focus of the movement is the tip of your chin.

Drop your head back slightly, but not all the way. Now, move your chin forward in a gentle circle, going out and away, down, around, and ending with your chin touching your chest. Just let your head and neck follow the movement.

Raise your head straight up, let it fall back slightly, then repeat.

Start out the nod very gently, with a very small circle. You will feel effort on the part of your neck muscles, but this is worked out as you nod and nod. Build up the circumference of your circle only after you feel you have dissolved the tension in your neck muscles.

The nod is a form of meditation, and even a half hour of nodding is not too much. To make it more interesting and more fun, accompany your exercise with some Middle Eastern or Indian music. Allow yourself to become lost in nodding—enter the land of Nod. When you finish, you'll feel beautiful.

Acupressure and Your Neck

Acupressure is the name for a form of Chinese acupuncture done not with needles but with the pressure of fingers. No one knows exactly how acupressure or acupuncture work, yet if you try it you'll see that there is a definite effect.

When doing the following techniques, bear in mind a proverb well known among acupressurists: "When working on the neck, proceed as if trying to slip past prison sentry guards." That is, start with extreme gentleness—don't barge in with a show of force, because there really is a "sentry guard" in the prison of your neck, and it will most assuredly attack you if you aren't very careful, and then you'll be back in prison for an even longer term than before. You *must* be gentle.

Here are six acupressure techniques to try:

On either side of the back of your neck you will find a long, powerful muscle. Starting at the top, where it joins your skull, press gently with the thumb. Hold

for a few seconds and release. Work your way down
slowly, covering the entire length of the muscle.

You will find that a headache is ordinarily accompanied by a knot in one of these two muscles.
Fool around until you find the knot (it will be tender)
and press it gently. Press and release over and over
until your headache fades—which it will.

Place the entire length of your thumb on the side
of your neck. Press firmly, and then run your thumb
down your neck from skull to shoulder in one smooth
motion. Repeat several times. Be sure to do *both*
sides, never just one.

At the top of your neck, in the middle, where it
joins the skull, you will find the *medulla oblongata.*
It's an important nerve center, a kind of second solar
plexus. With your thumb, push in and up on it fairly
firmly; hold for five seconds and release. Repeat
several times. This is a button you can push to clear
your mind. It also relaxes your entire body.

Raise your chin until your throat is stretched. Grasp
your Adam's apple with thumb and fingers. Press in
gently and move it from side to side. Then massage
the sides of it with up-and-down motions.

Hold your head with both hands. Lift it up off
your neck. Release. Repeat.

Find the ring of muscles at the boundary between
neck and head. Press it gently with the fingers across
its entire span. Release. Repeat over and over. Gradually increase pressure as the muscle softens.

Yawning, The Incredible
Relaxation Secret

Almost no one knows about the hidden power of yawning as a relaxation technique. In fact, to my knowledge, information about yawning has never before been made public.

It's no wonder that few know about the uses of a yawn, though, since there is virtually no understanding or agreement among medical scientists even about what a yawn *is*.

In 1971, after I had gone through a series of physical changes resulting from heavy use of some of the techniques in this book, my body began to change *itself* spontaneously. I would wake up in the morning and my thigh ligaments, for example, would literally ache to be stretched. Or my neck would want to be rolled, my feet would want to be massaged, my arms would want to do airplane spins. I went through different stages with my body—when one part seemed satisfied, another would rise up in need to take its place. A lifetime of tension was ready to be released. Fortunately, I knew or could invent techniques that could help my body accomplish this liberation.

Then, one day, I began to yawn. I yawned upon arising, as many of us do, but then I continued to yawn throughout the day. Sometimes it would reach a level of thirty to forty yawns an hour. I was taking classes at New York University at the time, which was lucky. The lectures were so large no one noticed my yawning.

The experience was so unusual that I was concerned lest something had gone wrong with me—this despite the fact that every yawn seemed to leave me fresher, more wide awake, more relaxed, and *softer*. A yawn is tremendous exercise for the whole face, too, and it appeared to me that my features were becoming more defined—clearer, more benign, and, frankly, more esthetically pleasing. Still, the experience was so bizarre that I resolved to research yawning to find out whether I had stumbled upon something wonderful or, on the contrary, I was in the grip of an unusual pathological symptom.

I read as much as I could, but it appeared that the yawn had never seemed worth writing about. Gurdjieff claimed that yawning was a way of sending energy from "the major energy reservoir" to the "minor energy reservoir," which sounded like a lot of mumbo-jumbo to me—he was never explicit about the location or operation of these so-called reservoirs. A man named Harvey Jackins, who had invented co-counseling techniques, described the yawn as one of the primary release mechanisms for repressed emotion. This seemed to jibe with my own intuition, but he still was unable to *define* a yawn. He could only describe, and speculatively at that, its possible function.

I then began to consult physicians and psychiatrists. None of them knew very much about yawns, nor did anyone seem to think they were very important. One doctor told me that yawns were the body's way of getting more oxygen. I asked him why, if one needed more oxygen, one didn't simply breathe more deeply spontaneously. He looked at me dumbly for a moment—me, an annoying and ignorant layman—and said, "Well, that's all we know about it."

I tried intensive deep-breathing methods. They made me yawn all the more! Clearly there was some gap in our knowledge about this natural phenomenon. I decided to collect the facts I could get, study yawns some more, and see what conclusion I could come up with myself.

Here is what I found:

Yawning is universal—certainly not to the degree that I was doing it, but we all yawn.

We are taught to cover our mouths when we yawn as if it is something impolite, and to "frame" our yawns—not let them grow too large. This seems to be a Western cultural phenomenon, since body functions can be positive ways to communicate in other cultures. (Belching after a meal is a great compliment in Japan, for example.) Since we live in a culture of emotional repression and Puritan physical shame, I reason that perhaps yawns are an extra-cultural form of emotional self-regulation.

A yawn stretches our jaw muscles and face muscles, in which we store a great deal of anger and anxiety.

Yawns are related to gagging and vomiting, which have been shown to be physical releasers of tension. In fact, if you hold a yawn wide open and keep your mouth open after the pull in your jaws is over, another yawn will follow, and eventually you will induce a gag or vomiting.

The classic yawn situations occur when we are bored or tired. These are both moments when we are, basically, disconnected emotionally.

Yawning a great deal makes *me* feel clear-headed, more relaxed, calmer, and more *wide awake*. (Try to notice your yawning; it probably does the same for you.)

We all feel at least a little relieved after a yawn.

It seems clear that a yawn is one of your body's natural tension releasers. You yawn when you're tired in order to get rid of the tension in your body that would otherwise keep you from getting to sleep or getting a complete rest when sleeping. That's why a yawn is a signal for sleep—it's a message from your body that it wants to do something about its fatigue.

You may also yawn in a boring situation. Usually when you're bored you experience a lack of interest *combined* with a circumstance that prevents you from leaving the boring situation. Thus a conflict is created, hostility and anger are aroused, and your body becomes tense, contracted. The only way you can remain in the situation without contracting even more is to somehow release the physical tension. For this reason you stretch and fidget when bored—and you yawn.

There are other times when you yawn seemingly for no reason. Even if you've had enough sleep and you're not particularly bored, yawning may begin spontaneously. Most people have experienced this kind of "eruption" several times. It passes, and no more is thought of it. This instance of yawning, too, is the body's natural reflex toward relaxation, and it occurs when you are being made tense by subconscious anxieties.

If you can yawn at will, by opening your mouth as wide as possible and holding it until a yawn appears, so much the better. If you can't, wait till the next time you yawn and try to carry it forward into developed yawning experience. Yawn not once, not twice, not three times, but as many times as you can over a quarter- or half-hour period. Just keep yawning again and again.

Keep your mouth open wide—it will help the yawns repeat themselves. Tilt your head backward—that's the natural position for a yawn. *Don't* cover your mouth—sit on your hands if you have to. Don't "frame" your yawn—let your mouth open as wide as it can and don't try to end the yawn before it is full and complete. (Most people are habitual framers, so this may take some work.) If you should experience a gag reflex, just let it happen—gagging is a good tension releaser.

Your eyes may tear; that's a good sign too. Yawn and yawn and yawn. You can do it in a special session, while driving, while traveling, even while walking. It's a strange experience, admittedly, and one that you've never tried, but the results are nothing short of amazing. Yawning alone can take you from a shut-down state of deadness and contraction into a frame of mind that is open, clear, vital, awake, and alive.

No one believes in the power of extended yawning from merely hearing or reading about it. You've got to take the plunge and try it with an open mind. Yawning works. Can anything be said more plainly?

Jumping for Joy

Frogs and kangaroos and rabbits jump—it's the only way they have to get around. We jump too, but we don't need to—jumping has no apparent survival value for us. Still, we jump nearly as soon as we can walk, and we do it in a variety of circumstances.

Kids jump up and down when they're happy or excited or sometimes just because they like doing it. Athletes jump (and slap!) when they make the crucial point—hit the home run, score the touchdown, bowl the strike. Contestants on game shows can hardly be restrained when they answer the question that wins them the brand-new Camarro. Africans jump rhythmically in their sensuous ritual dances; so do American Indians. When we're having a terrific party, the whole joint really jumps all night long.

It should be apparent that jumping is an expression of happiness, triumph, or excitement, and a way of releasing tension, usually the tension of suspense.

By consciously performing the behavior that's appropriate to happiness or tension release, we can experience the related feelings—that is, by doing something we do when we're happy we can actually become happier, much as we can slow down our total consciousness by slowing down our breathing. And by miming an act of release we can ease contractions that are lurking about deep within us, ease tensions of which we might not even be aware. Many of us have lost the ability to trigger this simple and joyous release, but it's easy to retrieve.

As with the other exercises, learn how to do this first as a ritualized technique, and then add your own variations (whatever feels good!). Jump not just during an exercise period but any time you sense a need for it in your legs. Add it to your personality; add it to your daily life. When you feel happy or when you are freed from suspense, go ahead and jump. Jump whenever the mood strikes you.

Here is a jumping exercise:

1. Start with your feet about fourteen inches apart. Your knees should be somewhat bent, your pelvis thrust forward, back straight and chin up. Make fists with your hands and place one over the other out in front of your chest. Now do a pantomime of someone riding a horse. Post up and down. Keep your feet flat on the floor.

2. As you're posting, try to feel all the parts of your body—especially your torso, shoulders, neck, and

head—and let them go looser. Your shoulders should bounce up and down. Your head should bobble on your floating neck. Let your hands begin to dangle off your wrists and move as they want to whenever you move. Get yourself, your whole body, loose and flowing.

3. Now spread your arms out like an eagle, posting all the way. Let them push up and down like giant wings. Let your hands dangle and jig. Keep posting, now deeper and smoother and lower. Feel your thighs. Feel your calves. Feel your feet.

4. Raise your arms up over your head. Point your fingers to the sky. You're still posting, but you're like a rocket ship and you're about to take off.

5. Start letting your feet come up off the ground as you post up. Gradually move into a real jumping action. *Exhale* each time you touch the ground.

6. Experiment. Jump off your toes. Jump off flat-footed, off your heels. Land soft. Land hard. Go really fast. When you get a little winded, don't stop, just slow down till you regain your strength. Jump for joy. *Exhale* when you land. Jump all around the room.

You should be in the actual jumping phase for at least two solid minutes (preferably longer) the first few times. Build up your time and endurance. Learn how to feel yourself and pace yourself. You really needn't stop when you're tired even though it seems necessary. Try just slowing down.

When you finally do stop, stop dead in your tracks. Let your arms fall. *Don't move.* Just stand and feel the tingling—feel your body, the circulation, the energy flow. See if there are any changes, any new tight spots or new spots of heightened feeling. Make a note of where they are so you can work on those areas

127

later—often when you're open you'll feel things that mysteriously disappear only a few minutes or hours later. We tend to close up fast.

Now lie in the corpse pose for five minutes. If possible, elevate your legs slightly to restore a normal distribution of blood. Think about the feelings and memories that jumping brought up in you. Feel how your body has aged, and try to remember your young body.

True Dance

We are very lucky to live in a time when we may dance in an extremely "primitive" way, unencumbered by the clutch of a necessary partner. Our dancing, like ourselves, is far less rigid and armored than it was in former times; now dancing affords an opportunity for the raising of energy, the integration of mind and body, and social participation all at once.

But our dances—each of which has a name (for example, the Hustle, the Bump) that describes a *form* that you are, generally, to *perform*—are still not primitive enough. They are restricted by the forms you are supposed to follow. The dancer works at presenting the right *appearance,* the form of whatever dance is current. In this way, the mind dances the body, and the situation should be reversed. Your body should dance your mind or dance itself. True dance has nothing to do with appearance.

True dance is a rhythmic form of stretching and exercise movement originating in the body's own will to motility. Since no two bodies or psyches are alike, no two true dancers will ever dance the same dance. In fact, since our somatic equilibriums are always changing, it is likely that no true dancer will ever repeat his or her dance in exactly the same way.

True dance does not tell a story, and it does not have a specified and preordained appearance or set of movements that must be followed. The movements of true dance originate in the emotions locked into the dancer's body, and in the corresponding structure of muscular tension that yearns to be released. A true dancer, while dancing, has no awareness of anything at all except the feelings in his or her body. So, as we shall see, dance the force for which comes from within is a form of meditation.

And it is a therapy, a therapy for contracted bodies. Who doesn't feel better after dancing? Why is dancing, even the type proscribed by form, invariably a pleasant experience? There is something profound about dancing—to either an external rhythm or an inner one—that few have taken the trouble to explore.

We are beasts of rhythm. We breathe in a rhythm. Our hearts beat in a rhythm. Our speech has its own peculiar rhythms. When we walk, it is to the beat of our own inner drummer.

The world around us is a world of rhythm, too. The sun comes up, the sun goes down. The seasons turn. The waves lap against the shore. All is rhythm.

Dance is the rhythmic movement of the body, and in that sense, many things are dance. Walking is dance, sex is dance, even eating is dance. The rhythm may be obvious and strict or varying and complex, but there is always a rhythm. Even the way you read is rhythmic and is a kind of dance.

The dance that emerges from within is the sort of dance that is therapeutic—that relaxes contracted muscles and releases energy, that clarifies the mind.

You can do it with the accompaniment of music or without. What's important is developing a flow of rhythm in exercising areas of your own particular body. Looks are unimportant. In fact, your dance may end up looking quite bizarre, but, though you may look unorthodox on the outside, you will feel utterly graceful within.

By now you have learned a large number of body movements and body positions that help return you to yourself. In dance you put them all together, adding your own transitions and any other movements that seem, *feel,* especially suited to your own body.

Start by shaking out your body. Shake one leg, then the other, then your hips, chest, arms, head, and neck. Shake your entire body all at once, as if you were standing on a pneumatic drill.

Begin to dance as you normally would, with no particular purpose in mind. Let your attention go inward and feel your body from head to toe. Try to feel the areas of your body that are *not* dancing, that are excluded from your dance, as it were. These are the places that are blocked or that themselves function as blocks. Is your head held square on a rigid neck? Is your chest like cast iron? Are your feet stationed on the floor, your legs brittle, your arms awkward, your hands unused?

Start with the part of your body that you notice first as being a nonparticipant. Focus on it, and alter your movements so that *that* part dances, too. Build your dance around the loosening and mobilizing of the neglected area.

Then, when it has joined the rest of your body in dancing, locate the next part that needs exercising by letting your attention flow and feel until it is stopped by a block. Try to incorporate the first area you worked on into your "dancing out" of the next one, if you can.

The important thing to remember is that you must not let yourself be held back by inhibitions about what you might look like or by new and strange feelings that arise when you oil up your body's rusty parts. Take up each rigidity as you notice it, work it loose, then ask your body what remains to be done. That's not a figure of speech—your body will tell you, if you listen to it.

Don't leave one area for another until you feel ready. It's okay to spend your whole dance just getting a smooth movement, for example, into your hips, or graceful motion into your arms and hands.

Abandon yourself! True dance is not something to be looked at, is not a form that has specified standards that you must meet. True dance is a method of somato-psychic therapy, and its movements are dictated by the need to counteract tensions dwelling in your own body.

You might turn into a frog, or a chicken, or a cat, or some mythical combination of animals—or into nothing you can recognize. It doesn't matter. Just dance out every tense area and you'll be completely refreshed—refreshed as in made fresh again, made new.

If you have any trouble getting going, it's probably because you're worried, subconsciously, about appearances. You can slip your foot in the door by rhythmically performing some of the movement techniques outlined in the previous sections of this chapter. Start with a movement that's proved particularly effective for you, and let your body and your sensitivity to it take you from there.

The Walks of Life

The first few halting steps of an infant are a wonderful and magical moment—they mark the point at which the infant begins to enter the world of human beings. In fact, the first distinction between human beings and other primates is the ability of the former to stand upright on two legs and walk.

The many occupations of man are known as "walks of life," and perhaps this is no mere coincidence of language, since, to be sure, the banker walks differently from the construction worker who builds the bank, and from the artist who rarely visits it, and from his wife who wishes he would spend less time in it.

It is among the most common facts of our common knowledge that a person's personality (not to mention station in society) is reflected in the manner in which he or she walks. We all have a typical method of locomotion—habitual, unconscious, a part of our very bone marrow—that tells the story of our attitudes and our feelings about ourselves and our world like an open book.

If we're aggressive, we walk with hard-heeled assertion (consider the German goose-step). If we crave attention we walk in noisy shoes, exaggerate our movements and gestures. The retiring person who feels inferior slouches. The unhappy person who feels oppressed and shut off from his or her desires shuffles. The whore has her own special walk. The effete person minces, as if he or she does not quite feel secure in touching the ground. The happy child skips or dances. The victorious or triumphant walk with their heads held high, while the beaten walk with their heads hung low. Walks may be awkward or elegant, but they are always eloquent.

As in jumping for joy, we can use our ability to imitate the physical manifestations of an emotional state to get new information about ourselves and our relations to others. Anyone can imitate a wide variety of walks and feel the variety of new feelings that go along with them. A particular walk is the result of an emotional state, and by imitating it we can uncover and loosen armor, experiencing as we go the element of those we imitate that exists inside each of us.

First, take an ordinary stroll and try to experience what your own walking is *really* like. Most of us never notice our own walks because our attention is focused on where we are going, where we are coming from, or what we are seeing on the way. Ourselves? We forget about ourselves.

How does your foot hit the ground? Heel first? Flat? Toe first? Soft? Do you feel a reverberation in your spine as your foot makes contact? Do you push off on your step with a long powerful stroke or a halting jerk? Feel your calves. Feel your knees. Do you walk from your knees or from your hips? Feel your thighs as you walk, and your hips and pelvis. Feel the set of your lower spine, the curve or straightness as it goes up, the angle of your neck where it joins your head. Are your eyes down, up, or straight even the least bit? How do your shoulders and chest sit? What do you do with your arms and hands? Which way do your palms face? Try to experience the totality of the way you walk in each and every part of your body. Make mental notes of the rigid or frozen parts, the parts that do not seem to be walking along with you, the parts that are merely there for the ride.

Walk *slowly* to bring yourself into better focus.

Now, as you walk slowly, try to integrate the immobilized parts. If your arms don't swing, let them. If they swing excessively try to relax those muscles, to tone down the movement. Feel the soles of your feet and try to roll across their entire length with your weight. Feel the movement of the muscles in your buttocks and the backs of your thighs and bring those muscles into play, exaggerating if necessary.

Go out and take a walk. Avoid thinking about where you're going or how far away from home you are. Just take a free and easy wander. Focus all your attention upon the mechanics of your walking. Move so that you compensate for and correct dead or armored areas of your body. Watch where you're going, of course, but pay attention only to your walking. This exercise creates a surprisingly vast change in your perception of the relationship between yourself and your environment, and between yourself-as-you-are and yourself-as-you-might-be. As such, it is really a form of moving meditation.

(To really blow your mind go to a fast-paced urban area and walk focused on your walking, *in slow motion.*)

When you have become familiar with the inner dynamics of your own walk and how it relates to your personality, it's time to try out the walks of others, the walks of life.

You will find that although you have one typical or habitual walk, you also modify your walk depending upon your emotional state. You may have, at times, a more elated, aggressive, withdrawn, depressed, threatening, subservient, feminine or masculine walk. When you impersonate other types of walking you will see that each type is an exaggeration of qualities that you yourself display from time to time. That's because there's a little of everyone in everyone. Even when you despise someone you despise him because you see in him something you recognize, a potential for something in your own character structure. After all, everyone you know is human. The personality of each of us is made up of the heightening of certain human traits and the suppression of others.

Try some of these "walks of life" and *exaggerate* the movements so you can fully experience what the walkers of *these* walks experience physically. If you really get into it, you will feel yourself experiencing the walks emotionally as well.

1. your father
2. your mother
3. your brother or sister
4. your mate or lover
5. one of your grandparents
6. your boss or teacher
7. fellow employees or students whom you like or dislike strongly
8. a construction worker
9. a serious businessperson
10. a professor
11. a waitress
12. a policeman
13. a prostitute
14. a mailman
15. an elderly person
16. an infant just learning how to walk
17. a four-year-old
18. someone skipping
19. a Mafioso type
20. a soldier
21. the President of the United States
22. a long-legged bird (don't forget wings)
23. a hairy gorilla
24. a walking tree
25. walking water
26. whatever you can think of

Now take another walk in your own personality. This time try to be as relaxed as possible. Let your shoulders drop down, let your stomach relax, let your buttocks fall, let your knees bend slightly. Send all the weight in your body down into the ground. Feel the ground beneath your feet; feel its solidity, feel the way you grow up from it. Imagine that there is a tremendous magnet attracting your feet to the ground, making it difficult to lift them, making them want to be in touch with the ground firmly and solidly. Imagine that your feet have an intense sexual attraction to the ground. Relax. Send your entire consciousness to your feet. Come down to earth, come all the way down to earth!

Dervish Whirling

In the early thirteenth century, Jalal al-Din Rumi, the great Persian poet, teacher, and Sufi master, encountered by chance a wandering dervish to whom he was powerfully and mysteriously attracted. He took this stranger, Sharus Al-Din, to his house and they became inseparable, involved in a constant communion lasting nearly two years. Rumi's disciples were cut off from their master's teaching during this time, however, and they greatly resented his devotion to Sharus Al-Din. The disciples threatened Sharus and he fled to Damascus. He returned and the disciples repented, but then their jealousy reared its hoary head once more with renewed bitterness. This time Sharus Al-Din fled without leaving a trace behind.

Rumi was emotionally thunderstruck by his contact with this "hidden saint," whom he felt was the perfect image of the wholeness, or god, or Beloved, for which he had spent his life seeking. He became an ecstatic poet, pouring forth verse in torrents. And to symbolize, it is said, the search for the lost Beloved (god, wholeness, unity, life-force, etc.) now identified with Sharus Al-Din, he invented the famous whirling and circling dance for his Mevlevi dervishes. This is performed to the accompaniment of the lamenting reed-pipe and the pacing drum.

Dervishes do the whirling dance all night long. They enter states no ordinary person has ever dreamed of. I have seen highly reputable documentary films showing the dervishes plunging swords through their cheeks and ribs with no evidence of bleeding. This they do to demonstrate the distance they have traveled from ordinary mortal weakness while moving in their inexorable circles.

It is possible to create a fascinating and valuable experience through dervish whirling on your own, with or without the accompaniment of music. We can forego the "proof" of experience that the dervishes use. There is no danger in whirling if it's done properly—you can whirl for an amazingly long time with absolutely no dizziness, and in fact little children whirl spontaneously all the time. (One recent study found that over eighty percent of the third-graders in the Walnut Valley, California elementary school system reported that they whirled frequently.)

In whirling you become like the earth, your center becomes like the earth's center. All around you becomes a turning fluidity. Only you, in the direct center, are stable and conscious. When you "return" from whirling you feel calm, and you sense the insignificance of the things that usually upset you emotionally. You become centered, solid, and real, immune to the illusions that try to buffet you and take you away from yourself.

Find a large open space with a smooth floor, like a gymnasium. (Don't whirl outdoors at first—the uneven ground presents too many difficulties for a beginner.) Stand with your feet about twelve inches apart. Raise both arms to shoulder height and extend them outward so your body makes the shape of a cross. Turn your right palm down to face the earth; turn your left palm up to face the sky. If you find it comfortable, tilt your head over and rest it lightly on your right shoulder.

Now begin to turn by taking a step around with your left foot. Keep the ball of your right foot planted and *pivot on the right foot.* Continue to step around with your left foot and pivot on your right until you develop a smooth turning motion.

In the beginning, at least, keep your eyes closed. Develop a speed that's comfortable for you—there's really no relationship between speed and effectiveness.

Here is the point that you must, repeat *must,* remember: *Never stop whirling abruptly. Always slow down gradually, very gradually, until at last you are taking baby steps and barely moving.* (Your body and your sense of balance will tell you just how gradual this gradualness must be.) If you try to slow down too fast you will become dizzy and fall, and you may become sick. If you slow down gradually, you will feel perfect.

Relax when you are whirling. There's no danger if you follow the directions. Breathe smoothly and deeply. Feel your body as it whirls—your feet, your legs, your hips, your arms, your head. Feel how distinct it is from your surroundings. Concentrate on the difference between "you in here" and "it out there." There is a very great difference, just as in other states you may realize there is a very great similarity. You need to experience both—the difference and the sameness between the you and all-that-is-not-you—if you wish your experience to have a close relationship to reality.

Slow Motion

All our vices come from sloth and impatience. And sloth comes from impatience.
—Franz Kafka

You have probably noticed that most of the techniques in this chapter call for slow motion in at least one phase of their performance. The reasons for this may already have become obvious through your own experience, but even if this is true slow motion deserves some additional attention because of its extreme importance.

There used to be a slogan about the amphetamine-methadrine group of drugs (which hype you up on nervous, rather than organic, energy) that said, "Speed kills!" And it's true about more than "speed," the drug—it's true about speed, the life-style. It's true about our personal habits and our ways of thinking, and it's perhaps most outstandingly true that speed kills in our relationship to our bodies. Speed perverts energy. Speeding, we cannot feel properly; our feelings are blocked. When we can't feel, we can't be real —we are, in effect, dead, dead from speed.

The more nervous you are, the faster and less gracefully your body moves. Your foot taps unconsciously, or you beat a tattoo with your fingers, or you scratch your head. You have a quick temper. You are upset by little things so fast you don't even have the chance to observe them and see your irrationality. In fact, your entire unconscious is made up of painful or fearful moments that entered you with so much speed that you couldn't stop them or deal with them rationally.

When you are tense, your heart beats fast, your blood pressure increases, your electrical charge—measured, for example, by lie-detector devices—increases, your bloodstream is flooded with abnormal amounts of adrenalin and other hormones, and your very brain waves undergo a marked and measurable alteration. It is no coincidence that such "civilized" problems as heart disease are virtually unknown in primitive areas where people are still close to themselves and the earth.

But you needn't beat a hasty retreat to the nearest Pacific island. There are ways, as you have been discovering, of returning yourself to "normal"—to a normalcy that is virtually unknown among the neurotic, busy, hyped-up people in our urban culture. You can return to your feelings, return to your body, return to your original energy. And those three "returnings," which are actually only one, are the key to happiness.

Slowing down is of the utmost importance. You *can* slow down in your life. You can arrange for less input and stimulation. You can refuse to rush when you're "running late"—what does a few minutes *really* matter? You can try to remember yourself, try to become more and more aware of your feelings and your energy system as you live your life—no matter how frantic it is.

The problem with trying to slow down is that you can't know the real meaning of slowness—can't know just *how* slow slow can really be—until you've experienced it directly. You must show your body and your mind what genuine slowness is, for they have forgotten. You must give them examples to follow, show them that slowness feels *good* so they will develop a taste for it, will want more and more of it.

And you need to give yourself a chance to feel yourself. When a magician does a card trick at top speed he will baffle you completely—you won't know what's going on. If he performs the same trick slowly you will see what he does, you will catch a glimpse of that card that was slipped out of the deck while your attention was diverted by his patter. The same is true of the magic tricks of your own psyche. The hand is sometimes quicker than the eye, to be sure. But the unconscious is infinitely quicker than the hand or anything else you've experienced. If something frightens or pains you, your body will contract in literally no time at all.

What is needed, then, is a way of reversing the contraction of the body and a way of experiencing life, in its smallest details, more slowly. Slow motion does both. It improves the quality of most stretching techniques, it slows down movement so that you can experience the personal meaning of your body's actions, and it provides a learning environment for developing the ability to slow down input when it arrives inside you.

141

Walk in slow motion. Experiment with different lengths of stride. (There's no better thigh exercise than a long-stride, slow-motion walk.) As you walk, concentrate on the soles of your feet. Imagine that there is a sticky glue on them, or that gravity has become suddenly more powerful than ever before. Walk with your feet intensely attracted to the ground.

Don't forget to use your arms, hands, and torso just as you would while walking normally. The only difference is that now every part of your body should be slowed down.

Slow motion can be almost painful—not in the ordinary sense of physical pain, but because of the high degree of discipline and patience required. When doing slow motion, always try to go beyond the point at which you don't think you can do any more. That's when the potency and the power of the exercise multiply.

Eat an entire meal in slow motion.

Enact a social situation—the moment of greeting someone, for example—in slow motion.

Lying on your stomach, pantomime swimming in slow motion.

Become angry in slow motion.

Smile and then wipe the smile off your face in slow motion.

Imitate a flying eagle or an octopus in slow motion.

Do any of the exercises in this book that attract you, but do them as slowly as you possibly can.

Experiment and develop your own slow-motion situations depending upon the needs of your own body.

Make love—in slow motion.

Remember, keep your body flowing and graceful, your movements continuous, your mind focused, and your feelings tuned to the experience.

Manual Labor

In almost everyone's lives there are chores that simply have to be done, and these chores are looked upon as a burden. But you can relax, meditate, and generate energy as you get the job done by applying the energizing principles of romantic exercises to your ordinary physical labor. Some examples:

Sweeping: Build up a rhythm of small strokes, exhaling each time you stroke, inhaling each time you place the broom in position. You can also combine this with neckwork, slow motion, and energy-sending poses.

Washing dishes: Take complete breaths. Soap on your inhale, rinse on your exhale. Make your movements even, smooth, and continuous. Place dishes in the rack in slow motion. Stand back from the sink so you stretch your calves, thighs, abdomen, shoulders, and forearms while washing. (You can do the same while ironing.)

Dusting: Hold your cloth with a claw. Send energy into it.

Chopping wood (an excellent exercise for chest and shoulder armor): Extend your arms high over your head on the downswing. Exhale vigorously on the chop.

Whatever the task, try to turn it from a necessary chore into an exercise that benefits you. The facts of survival do not necessarily militate against personal growth. As long as you have to do certain things, you might as well have fun and add to yourself in the process.

Finding Your Own Ways of Movement

A fundamental precept of personal or consciousness development is that there is no one method suitable for everyone. In this chapter you have been shown many examples of techniques that are time-tested and based on the logic of the body. Though we are the same in the sense that we all have bodies and minds, we are also each unique and individual. Each of us is armored in different ways, and, if you seek release, you need to experiment and explore to find which of the given exercises work best for you. Beyond that, you need to discover what variations may make a relatively weak technique powerful *for you*.

The difference between effectiveness and ineffectiveness can be very slight. It might mean leaning forward slightly, or back, or changing the angle of your limbs a few degrees, or altering your posture slightly. The difference might be as small a detail as spreading your fingers or curling them into a fist, or standing on your toes instead of your heels.

There are things you have got to discover for yourself. What you have learned so far is a kind of language. To become fluent you need to practice and you need to try to create your own "sentences." Don't be bound by the instructions I've given. Feel free to "grow your own" exercises based on the principles that have been demonstrated. All it takes is a sensitivity to your body, a sending of your mind and energy all around it to discover the locations of your blockages. Use the somatic vocabulary you have learned and your own uninhibited imagination to release them. When you do, you'll know it. You'll feel it.

This process is called finding yourself.

Chapter Six

Meditation and Deep Relaxation

The mind is a cruel master but a useful servant.
—Ramana Maharishi

THERE HAS BEEN MUCH WRITING AND TALK about meditation recently, and many attempts have been made to define it. Meditation has been called deep yet animate rest, one-pointedness, no-pointedness, the practice of inner peace, self-hypnosis, prayer, the creation of alpha-waves, and the experience of nothingness. In a sense, all of these labels contain some truth, but none is a broad enough definition. The reason for this, of course, is that there are many ways to meditate and a variety of resulting effects. Meditation is like a house with many doors—each admits you, but from each you will take a different pathway to get to the kitchen.

One thing is certain. The experience of meditation is different from any other conscious experience we can have. In fact, it is so different that—though we can have awareness and memory of what has happened—it cannot be likened to any other conscious moment. It straddles the unknown area between consciousness and unconsciousness.

Your ordinary conscious state is subject to many changes depending on the condition of your individual psyche and your environment. On the contrary, the meditation state, in the words of renowned Zen scholar D. T. Suzuki, "attains a state of uniformity or sameness or equilibrium." This state is without tensions, worries, fears, anxieties, fantasies, thoughts about the future, memories of the past, calculations, wishes, or dreams. If you can imagine all these thoughts and emotions as little objects that occupy a space in your mind, meditation is the experience of the space *without the objects in it*.

Imagine an eel in your bathtub, incessantly swimming and roiling about in the water. Now imagine taking it from the water and tossing it out the window. It hasn't disappeared—it's just not *there* anymore. Now look back at the water, clear and calm and motionless. The eel is your psyche. The water is your energy system—that which exists when all that you can think of or imagine has been removed.

The effect of a proper meditation is utter and complete relaxation of your body, of your whole metabolism, and this can be achieved in no other way. In the current literature on meditation you will find reputable scientific studies demonstrating that all those funny-looking monks and Yogis who put forth meditation as a means to a better life were right, hundreds of years before the first electroencephalogram.

As we have seen, relaxation of the contracted body allows energy to flow—that's why people who take up the practice of relaxation report greater energy in their lives when they're *not* meditating, and why a meditation period always makes them feel even more refreshed and optimistic.

For a really full energy flow, somatic exercise is not enough—meditation is necessary, too, to raise your energy level. But meditation *alone,* helpful as it may be, is not the answer either. Here is where the highly commercialized transcendental meditation movement has missed the heavenly boat. If you are tense or contracted or blocked by character armor when you meditate, that condition will interfere with the heights to which you can go. It may even prevent you from realizing any benefit from meditation at *all.* Somatic techniques, then, bring you to a plateau of energy from which the next ascent is through meditation.

In the previous chapter, you learned to feel yourself and your energy in various specific aspects. Meditating, you will learn to feel yourself *without* this specificity. You will feel yourself as pure self, as self and self alone—and as self as a conduit for an energy that is mysterious, but is clearly larger than you yourself or any of us.

Through the process of relaxing and feeling your energetic nature, your energy will itself increase. Your potential energy becomes manifest and realized both when you are meditating *and* afterwards, as you live your life. The more you meditate—in conjunction with practicing the other techniques—the more energy you will have.

This energy we're talking about is not nervous or

manic or driven energy. It is calm, beautiful, creative, powerful, self-nourishing, self-perpetuating energy. It is the energy of one no longer bounced like a tumbleweed on the winds of the emotions, the energy of a continuously strong and clear-headed state, the energy of "equilibrium."

It has been mentioned many times that thoughts and emotions resulting from or creating a contracted body are the prime obstacles to the experience of freely flowing energy. Many people, though, are unaware of exactly what is meant by "thoughts" and thus are unable to recognize their own states, their own consciousness. When you get very quiet, in meditation or in deep relaxation, you will begin to perceive that you are constantly talking to yourself. You are wondering about what you are doing, what you were doing before, what you are going to do later. All the ruminations are subsconsciously— sometimes consciously—verbalized.

When you begin to meditate, you will find that all these things come to the fore as you become still. (This is much the same as the flood of images and thoughts that come to you just before falling asleep.) You must become extremely aware of the existence of this form of mental activity, for the degree of its absence is to become your yardstick for measuring the effectiveness or depth of your meditation.

Some say you can only cause "noise" to cease by an act of will. Some say you need to be aware of it but not to act upon it. Some say you must focus only on the meditation techniques and pay absolutely no heed to "mental noise." All the options will be presented; how you decide to deal with "noise" is up to you. Perhaps you will want to create a blend of all three ways to handle it, or develop a new, more subtle approach. It doesn't matter. What matters is that you realize the difference between merely sitting still for a period of time, and meditating. Meditating changes you. Stillness alone does not.

A note on simplicity: Because meditation is a new phenomenon to large numbers of Americans, there is a curious desire among many to have it be highly mysterious and complex. You are not required to have a guru to learn meditation, and you are most emphatically not required to pay hundreds of dollars for a personal mantra in a language you do not even understand. Meditation involves a single simple principle— learning to relax your body and quiet your mind. The means to this end are techniques involving repetition, one-pointedness, mindfulness of breathing, and the paradoxical "will to let go." These means turn out to be rather humble and practical, not magical, and they are within the reach of anyone.

Never pass by a meditation technique just because it seems too simple or unsophisticated—it may be perfect for your own temperament. Some methods work for some people, some don't, and no one seems to know why. But it's a good idea to try each one at least a few times, to see what suits you. There is no hierarchy of complexity, really, no progression from "beginner's" meditation to "advanced." The ordinary can work just as well as the unusual.

Posture in meditation is not too important, though you will probably obtain the best results from sitting upright with your back unsupported. Following are several techniques for meditation self-taught.

Mindfulness of Breathing

Awareness of breathing can be a part of your meditation technique, or it can become a total method by itself. It provides a repetitive action—the constant inhaling and exhaling—and one-pointedness through keeping the mind on a single thing that has no external purpose. The slowing of your breathing and/or concentration upon it also seems to have an intrinsic power to relax the entire system; why this should be so is not easy to explain, but there it is.

A noted Tibetan Buddhist teaching in this country recommends mindfulness of *breathing only* as the only way to meditate, and Zen Buddhists and some Hindus find breath-counting effective. Attention on breathing certainly internalizes you, removes you from the distractions of the external world. This internalization quiets the mind and gives you an excellent opportunity to observe yourself and hear (in its slowed-down, dissipated mode) your inner noise. It also gives you a good opportunity to explore your subconscious and discover what forces are really controlling you, and it helps you to relax and empty yourself at the same time.

Mindfulness

Simply become aware of your breathing. Don't try to change it—just observe it and feel it. But *do* be careful to *keep* your mind on your breathing, because your mind will want to wander. When it does, note what has been going on and return to a consciousness of breathing. There's no need to scold yourself or lurch back from your wandering—accept it as a natural phenomenon.

Retain your mindfulness of breathing at least fifteen minutes at a time, preferably an hour. Many things can happen when you do this, for a tight lid is not clamped on the subconscious. It will want to rise up and take over your activity, as it does all the time in ordinary life. Expect the unexpected.

Breath Counting

Taking ordinary breaths or complete breaths, count each one. You may count groups of ten or count continuously. When you experience a thought or an emotion, anything other than the consciousness of counting or the feeling of relaxation—*when you talk to yourself,* in other words—you should go back to number one. In this way you will see your ability to concentrate gradually increase as you are able to count further and further before "faltering."

Note that either technique can be used in almost any situation in your daily life, without anyone else being aware of what you are doing—your eyes may be open or closed, it doesn't matter.

"Weight"—A Trick from Self-Hypnosis

Self-hypnosis is very similar to meditation—the primary difference is that self-hypnosis makes practical use of the relaxed, vulnerable state to effect attitudinal change in your subconscious. Experts in self-hypnosis have developed a method of relaxation they call "deepening" that can be grafted onto meditative practice with extraordinarily good results. I would recommend using this "weight" technique with any type of meditation you may choose to do. It's almost a meditation technique in itself, and will definitely enhance any other method. It is, in fact, the nicest way I know of to relax, somatically or psychically, and it works no matter how tense I am.

The principle behind "weight" is simple. Each time you exhale, imagine you are getting heavier. Let yourself sink deeper and deeper into a more relaxed state by getting heavier and heavier with each exhale. Imagine yourself sinking through the floor if you are lying down, or sinking through the chair if you are sitting. Imagine that each exhale adds five pounds to your body weight. Exhale all your lightness. Become *heavy*. Return to the earth that is pulling you down. Feel the pull of gravity more and more as you go deeper and deeper, get heavier and heavier. Feel the weight of atmospheric pressure pushing down on you, making you heavier and pushing you deeper; feel yourself becoming more and more relaxed as you go deeper and deeper, become heavier and heavier.

If you want a heavy meditation, add weight to it.

Clock Watching

Watching the clock is usually a sign of nervousness. The passage of time always seems too fast or too slow; the clock becomes a symbol of tension. Here is a way to relax, to concentrate, to meditate, using the very clock that is ordinarily so oppressive. It's a way to turn the tables on time, as it were, by becoming timeless.

You will need a clock or watch with a sweep second hand. Sit upright with the clock or watch face at eye level. Take some complete breaths and do some neck rolling to relax yourself.

Now fix your gaze upon the tip of the second hand. Follow it as it sweeps all around the clock face. Each time you exhale, feel your gaze focusing more and more intensely on the tip of the second hand. Also add weight with each exhale.

See if you can do this for two minutes without having any extraneous thoughts. If you have one, stop. Rest your eyes for a little while and try again. When you find your natural time period for concentration, establish that as your bare minimum. Work at increasing the length of time you can focus your attention without interruption. Your goal should be a thirty- to fifty-percent daily increase.

Clock watching is a good way to develop the powers of your mind for meditation, for sending energy, and for relaxing different parts of your body at will, without stretching. Most people experience an instant relaxation while doing it, and a positive sign is the sensation of energy streaming in your legs, face, or other part of the body.

The Doven

Orthodox Jews are often seen rocking back and forth during the chanting of prayers, and this repetitive movement provides the continuity that we are looking for in meditative practice. The fact that there is physical movement is not a detriment—constant movement that isn't strenuous often forms the basis for meditation technique. Recall that certain techniques in the previous chapter, most notably dervish whirling, were referred to as "moving" meditations. If you are a very physical and active person, a moving meditation may work best for you.

To doven, simply stand with your feet about eighteen inches apart and your hands clasped behind your back and rock to and fro. Start out with a gentle rocking and let it develop naturally. If you can, inhale on the backward rocking and exhale on the forward rocking. Also, you will get extra power if you repeat over and over, to yourself or aloud, a single syllable. This might be the classic "Om," or "la," or "hey," or "who." (You should do the same with dervish whirling, neck rolling, or slow-motion walking.) Perform your repetitive motion for at least fifteen minutes without interruption.

Be sure to concentrate totally on your activity and lose yourself in it. Find a single point to focus your attention upon, such as your feet in whirling, and *keep* it there, no matter what. These activities will bring a continuous state of energy equilibrium, and they are extremely useful when followed by a "still" meditation to take advantage of the harmonious state they develop.

The Third-Eye Lock

Many people find it is easier to meditate when they limit the activity of their eyes. There is considerable sense to this, for eye movement is often the key sign of—and the main reinforcement for—our emotional vacillation.

Meditation usually works best when the eyes are either fixed upon one object or temporarily "disconnected," but they should not be allowed to roam free. So, in techniques that do not actually use your eyes as part of the method, you may find it helpful to institute the third-eye lock. Contemplation of the so-called "third eye" place on the forehead is a part of many classic forms of meditation.

Raise your eyes as for the eye exercises described in the previous chapter. Imagine that you are looking at a point in the middle of your forehead. If your eyelids are open when you do this, you will see a shadowy V-shape that marks the center of your upper vision.

Keeping centered is important when you do the eye lock. Because the position is strange it may cause a little strain at first—rest if you feel this happening. After you have become used to it and your eye muscles have stretched out, however, you will find this an extremely comfortable position that you can hold literally for hours.

Since it limits the movements of your eyes, the third-eye lock limits your susceptibility to "mental noise" and extraneous thoughts. But don't attempt to lock in a *downward*-gazing position. The long-term effect is very demoralizing.

Gazing at the Tip of Your Nose

Gazing at the tip of your nose is a highly respected meditation technique often employed by the Buddhists of Tibet. It uses a physical one-point to yield up self-awareness and empty the mind. If gazing at the tip of your nose seems odd or even silly to you, you're making a fairly common mistake. Simple as it may be, this is one of the most potent methods of meditation known.

When you're distraught, when thoughts have led you far, far out of yourself, look at the tip of your nose. As one guru has said of this exercise, "The effect is certain. It calms the mind."

You can gaze at the tip of your nose at a specific time each day that you choose arbitrarily; while riding in a car, bus, or train; while walking; during "dead" waiting time; or whenever you need a peaceful state of mind.

To gaze at the tip of your nose, sit upright and quiet yourself by becoming mindful of your breathing. Now simply gaze at the tip of your nose! Don't strain your eyes or cross them, and be gentle with yourself —don't expect perfection the first time. Even if your focus is weak you will experience the calming effect of this exercise. You get a better "target" on the tip with practice and experience. Just remember not to strain your eyes —this isn't a competition, and you have to learn the technique gradually.

You'll no doubt discover that your mind, which doesn't like to be "harnessed" this way, will try to lead you away from the one-point. Don't become upset when this happens; just gently go back to it.

You may experience a tingling or a numbness running down the ridge of your nose; this is a good sign. When you feel this you are ready to do the meditation with your eyes closed, by focusing on the feeling on the top of your nose. Once you've attained the numbness you may feel it coming on spontaneously while you're in the middle of something else. If you possibly can, drop whatever you're doing and meditate on the tip of your nose. The deepest and most powerful meditation occurs when meditation itself calls you to do it.

More Gazing Techniques

The one-pointed focusing of your eyes has always proved effective in meditation. There are other techniques similar to those already mentioned that you may find more or less attractive, and, since it's important to know all the options, you should try them. Nothing is more valuable than a meditation method that works well *for you*.

Some tested gazing favorites are:

1. the head of a pin
2. a candle flame
3. the space *between* the leaves of a tree or plant
4. your hand
5. a religious image
6. a spot on the wall in the *center* of your vision
7. clouds
8. a star
9. a glass of water
10. a pond or puddle

Increase the force of your gaze with each inhale and add "weight" with each exhale. Any gazing exercise should be done for at least fifteen minutes at a time. The longer you go beyond that, the more interesting things you will discover about yourself.

Oral and Silent Mantras

Mantras are yet another way to attain inner continuity or equilibrium. The repetition over long periods of a single syllable, word, or phrase absorbs the mind and causes the body to relax. Repeating a mantra is a fairly effortless means of shutting off the emotional forces that create contraction and turning on the intuitive mechanisms of insight.

It should be remembered that turning off your emotions is not the goal here—the goal is finding ways of eliminating the defensive reactions to feelings that contract and deaden your body. Feelings themselves are natural and *should be felt*, but they must be felt as phenomena, as objects. They should *not* be your masters. The state of energy equilibrium obtained through the repetition of a mantra enables you to feel your feelings without being manipulated by them.

Oral and silent mantras have somewhat different effects, so you should do both in order to gain the benefits of each. The oral mantra, or chanting, vibrates your vocal apparatus and massages resonators throughout the torso. Besides producing a mental state of continuity, the oral mantra helps to dissolve armor by vibrating the body, promoting the free flow of inner energy.

How does this happen? Well, when we hear a sound, more than our ears is involved. To use a gross example, when you hear heavy bass notes from a stereo set, the noises resonate in your hips and legs. If you observe carefully, you will see that high notes resonate in your teeth and jaws. The same is true when you speak—higher or deeper notes resonate in different places in your body. It's possible to clear out your sinuses by producing the proper tones with "n" and "ng" sounds, and, in particularly open states, you can chant a scale that resonates every vertebra of your backbone—in order. There is a whole school of Yoga, Laya Yoga (that is, Sound Yoga), that is centered on the creative properties of sound.

Silent mantras are more subtle. Although they don't dissolve armor directly, they help relax the body as a totality. The silent mantra form of meditation is a way of one-pointing both your aural sense and your entire verbal mind. It is the least sensuous of the meditations so far presented in that no attention is directed to the body or to any sense organs, but it is certainly no less effective than any other.

There has been much talk lately about the magical effects of chanting certain Sanskrit words—transcendental meditation. However, the most recent scientific studies indicate that the mystic words have no more powerful effects than ordinary words. Still, it seems clear that any mantra will have its best effect if violent sounds like "fff" or "sss" are avoided. Large sounds and soft sounds, such as the classic mantra "Om" (pronounced with a long O), are always most soothing and relaxing, and there is no sense fighting the intrinsic qualities of language and speech sounds.

Chanting is simple, and you can do it anywhere, any time, even while cooking a meal or driving in rush-hour traffic. When anxiety attacks, stop and chant. Your tension will dissolve; problems will appear infinitely less important and less insoluble. Give your mind a rest and it will often spontaneously find a creative answer to your problems.

Repeat one of the following words or syllables over and over for at least fifteen minutes. If your mind wanders, gently return it to the mantra. Don't be angry at yourself for slipping up—just return to your mantra and do the best you can. With practice you will do it better and better and it will become an increasingly easy and enjoyable way to "stop the world."

Try several mantras, for they do have differing effects. Choose ones you like from the list below or invent your own. Meaning is unimportant; sound is everything. Permit your body to move as it pleases while you chant.

Oral Mantras

Om

Om Shanti

Om Mani Padme Hun

One

Hare Krishna

La; La Ka; Oh La

Hyan; Nyee; Nyoo (good for sinuses)

Gong (good for chest and sinuses)

Plane

Spool (good for lips)

Clear (good for lips)

Ya Ha Di

Allah Hu

Bee Lee Do

Silent Mantras

Om

Om Shanti

One

Love

Ritual

Floating Clouds

I Am One

Energy Coming

Nam Myho Renge Kyo

Seventeen Seventy-Six

Light Within

I Am Alive

Meditation with Imagination

There are numerous methods for meditating with the aid of visualization or imagination. The imagination can be a potent force for relaxation, energy arousal, and self-discovery. Here are some of the best-known techniques. You can use them as is or adapt them to your own tastes—imaginatively!

Object and Shape Visualization

Let's say that you've spent some time gazing (peacefully!) at the head of a pin. The next step in this type of meditation is to close your eyes and *visualize* the pinhead. The object is to develop a fully accurate, three-dimensional image of it, not merely a line of color. Don't strain, though—the more you relax, the easier it will be to develop an accurate image.

You can do this with a candle, a cross, or any other small object. Spend some time gazing at it, then develop an image with your eyes closed. Hold the image for a full meditation session. Remember, the more relaxed you are, the easier it will be to develop the image and to retain it for long periods of time.

The image provides a kind of check or test for the degree of your concentration and relaxation. If it fades or starts turning, you are either tensing up or becoming fatigued (the latter happens toward the end of a session). Start with five minutes on this technique and try to build up to half an hour. If you can hold an image steadily for thirty minutes, that's real inner power!

Another method many people have found useful is the visualization of a specific (though abstract) geometric shape. With your eyes closed and "locked" on the third-eye point, imagine a sharply defined circle (spinning, if you like) or a horizontal bar, or a diamond, or an S. Focus on the image, and then relax more and more by counting breaths and adding weight. Again, the more you relax the easier it will be to hold the image.

As with a silent mantra, if you lose the image don't become frustrated or angry, simply generate it and hold it once again. It is not a reflection on your character if you lose the image—it only reflects the fact that you allowed yourself to tense up for some reason. Relax, *relax*. Relax and enjoy!

The Foaming Light

This imaginative meditation is often taught by Pir Vilyat Inyat Kahn, current leader of the Sufis.

Sit upright and begin to calm yourself with deep complete breaths. Count your breaths and add weight with each exhale. Do this for about ten minutes, until you are fully quiet and open.

Now, as you exhale, imagine that a hole is gradually opening in the crown of your skull—just in the place where the skull is soft and open in a newborn baby. Imagine that all the tension and "waste products" of your inner spirit are flowing out through the hole. As you inhale, imagine you are inhaling all the good energy in the atmosphere, the energy of the sun.

As this energy enters you, there is a strange reaction. It acts like bicarbonate of soda in water—it creates a foam of light deep inside you. Continue to exhale through the "hole" in the top of your head, and, gradually, the foam of light will begin to spill out the hole. The foam builds and builds until it is a billowing wave flowing out and covering your head with silvery light, flowing down over your shoulders, slowly, like lava, flowing down and covering your entire body with foaming, dazzling light. Continue in this perfectly lovely state, all covered with light, until your source of foam runs dry.

There are some variations on the foaming light idea. Some people like to imagine colored fountains flowing out the "hole." I have had great fun imagining the growth of a "headdress" that started as a little sapling and became a graceful palm tree (no coconuts ever fell on my head). One of my students became utterly possessed with the fantasy that millions of bright red apples were flowing out from his "core."

Among people who reach a highly refined energy

163

state there is often the spontaneous arousal of the feeling of *having* a "headdress." Why this should occur is a mystery, but it has been reported fairly frequently. When you are in a special state many things can happen that defy explanation, rational *or* mystical. It is as if the inner energy has a natural drive toward liberating itself and does so whenever the opportunity arises. When you feel something unknown happening spontaneously, *do* go along for the ride. You are likely to wind up in a wonderful place that you could arrive at by absolutely no means other than this spontaneity.

The Thousand-Petaled Lotus Flower

Another meditation using the imagination involves forming an image (at the third-eye point) of a thousand-petaled lotus flower. This is a classic Hindu meditation. However, since I haven't a very good idea of what a thousand-petaled lotus flower looks like, I prefer to contemplate a white rose. Use whatever flower you like. And many other images will work too—try palm trees, rain, clouds, a sunset, tall green grass, swaying seaweed, the surface of a pond, etc. Choose one that is meaningful to you, that you associate with peace, tranquility, beauty, and love.

Meditation and Space

Attention to space—to its infinitude and ultimate ineffability—has been a standard in the repertoire of meditative practices over the centuries. After all, space is the basic "given" of all existence; we can imagine the absence of anything—of air, of the earth, of light—but we *cannot* imagine the absence of space. Our beings are predicated upon space, and, because we cannot imagine the absence of space, our whole way of thinking, feeling, and experiencing is infused with the concept and the reality of space.

Cut the space between any two points in half. Now cut it in half again. Continue to cut the space in half until the space is infinitesimally small. Obviously, you can never completely eliminate the space by decreasing its size by half. But if you carry this line of logic to its extreme, you will see that the space becomes *so* small that you can no longer imagine its existence. (What is half the width of an atom?) The space becomes so small that we have no scientific instruments to measure it—just as we have no instruments to measure nothing. Infinitely small space is beyond our ken, but we know it's there even if we can't measure it. (Our "knowledge" is really imagination—extrapolation.) Space can become so small that it passes beyond the range of our ability to measure or truly conceive it—yet we *cannot deny* that it is still there. We cannot imagine space to be *gone*, for the simple reason that in our reality it cannot be.

So, sit quietly, add weight, and imagine that the space you are in (e.g., the room) is shrinking and shrinking until it is infinitely small—beyond all measurement or imagining—and you are still inside that space!

The more conventional Hindu meditation on space concerns itself with infinite *largeness*. (Space is *bigger* than we can imagine, too.) Enter into a deep state of equilibrium and quiet by the techniques previously discussed. Then imagine that the room you are in is growing larger and larger. The size of a house, of a block, of a town, of a city, of a continent; the size of the earth, the size of all the universe, growing and growing and ever expanding into the unimaginable. And you are a part of that infinite space, that space in which you are always living.

Try to plant the experiences of infinite space and of infinitesimal space in your mind. Remember them as you live your daily life, for they will help you to gain a better perspective on your values and on the true relative significance of things. It may seem odd, but the development of your sensitivity to space can bring profound insight into what is important in this life and what is not.

Listening

Another way of meditating that is very similar to spatial meditation is listening. There are two ways to do this one—the outer way and the inner way. Each has the customary deeply restful benefits common to all meditations, but each is different. Outer listening tends to establish you in your space in this real and concrete world, while inner listening is a way of peering into your subconscious and discovering its contents. Both types of experience are important if you want an immersion in all that meditation has to offer.

Outer Listening

Sit in a comfortable chair and deepen yourself through breath counting and adding weight. Now begin to listen; listen deeply. Listen to the pressure of the air on your eardrums. Listen to the noises in the house. Listen to the moving air outside, and to the traffic or people or whatever else is outside. If you hear a sound, follow it as it comes closer and/or travels away from you.

Extend your listening outward, always outward, as in spatial expansion, until you are listening to things at such a great distance that you cannot possibly hear them. At this point, pay the utmost attention to anything you might hear. Even if you do not understand it, remember it. Understanding may come later. Try listening to California, for example, or Paris, or the White House. To the meditating mind, cities and other places are symbols, symbols that can have meaning and can "speak" to you of things you may already know but are unable to hear.

Inner Listening

Enter a meditative state. In this technique the goal is to open yourself to what is commonly referred to as the "Inner voice." Listen to your heartbeat, listen to your breathing. When you are very relaxed, start "listening" inside your feet. Allow your listening to slowly flow up your body and into your head. Listen to what's inside your own head.

This is a simple exercise, but you will be amazed at the number of times that a voice—a tangible, real voice—will speak to you. And it will often be a voice you don't quite recognize; sometimes it will be grotesque and rather frightening.

Remember what is said to you. It might be a message from your subconscious, or it might be a voice that reflects and is forced out by suppressed emotions within you (for example, you might hear your father's voice telling you to work harder, or your mother's telling you to be more beautiful, or both telling you to be less sexy). Try to decide whether what you hear is a message or a childish formulation of repression. The decision won't always be an easy one to make. Whatever the case, you will certainly learn more about yourself by listening.

Mind over Matter

By now you have learned how to relax deeply yet with awareness, and how to focus your mind one-pointedly. It is possible to relax even more deeply by "sending" your one-pointed mind throughout your body, relaxing parts of it or all of it at will.

Lie flat on your back in the corpse pose. Take complete breaths, slowly, and add weight. Feel yourself getting heavier and heavier with each exhale.

Now, to relax your body, simply focus your attention on any part. Take the inner route, traveling from your brain down through your torso and down through your legs if, for example, you want to relax your ankles or toes. Always take the inner route—don't try to jump from your head to the part you want to relax; instead, let energy flow to the area by virtue of your concentration. Your concentration, incidentally, should not be a straining effort—a mere focusing of attention is all that's required.

For the first few times, start with your toes and send your mind to every part of your body. Go slowly. Don't leave an area until it feels fully relaxed. A good way to measure relaxation is to imagine the unrelaxed parts of your body as white. When your attention is effortlessly focused upon a part, it will slowly turn black—the deep, open, crystalline black of the nighttime sky. Turn your entire body from white to black until you are a total blackness, empty, calm, almost without a body at all.

(Don't forget to relax your neck, face, and head.)

Deepening

To insure that your meditation is as complete as you can make it, try borrowing this method from self-hypnosis.

As you are relaxing, as you are slowly breathing with awareness and getting heavier and heavier with each exhale, imagine that you are in a grade-school classroom, sitting at your desk. As you look at the blackboard, a large number 10 appears. With your next exhale a number 9 appears, and as it appears you become heavier, sink deeper, becoming more and more pleasantly relaxed. With your next exhale a number 8 appears, and you become still more heavy and relaxed. Continue these descending numbers, becoming deeper and more relaxed with each one, until you reach zero, at which point you should be far deeper into a meditative state of animate relaxation than you have ever been before. When you see the 0 appear on the blackboard, allow yourself (your imagining self) to float up from your desk and then up toward the blackboard. Pass through the blackboard through the hole in the zero. Pass into a floating cloud of infinite blackness and allow yourself to float freely and aimlessly until something happens. (It will.)

Whenever you feel yourself departing from the meditative depths, use this deepening technique to return there. If you like, you can also imagine yourself walking down the stairs of a ten-story building, or even sliding down a curving tube with ten loop-the-loops. Many images will work; the basic concept is a numerical descension upon which your attention is riveted, and which carries with it a preordered suggestion of relaxation.

As you will learn with practice, there is virtually no limit to the degree to which you can relax with awareness. No matter how relaxed you get, how deep you go, you can always go deeper. And depth is not merely a change in quantity—it can become an extraordinary change in quality as well. But that remains for you to discover.

A Total Meditation

Many people have neither the time nor the inclination to try out many forms of meditation to see which works best for them. They want a meditation that will work with instructions that they follow. With the caveat that it seems unlikely that any one meditation will serve all people equally well, I will here present a "total meditation" made up of features contained in the previous meditations in this chapter. This meditation has yet to completely fail anyone who tries it.

First read the instructions until you know them well. It makes no sense to interrupt a meditation in the middle to go back and look up what comes next.

1. Sit on the edge of a chair with your back straight but not rigid. Open your eyes as wide as you can, focus them on a single spot on the opposite wall, and do the Yogic cleansing breath (a series of short exhales through a puckered mouth after a complete inhale).

2. Close your eyes and do some neck rolls. Chant

a long "Om" sound as you roll your neck. After the neck rolling, flex every muscle in your body (*every* one) all at once, hold, and relax all at once.

3. Gaze at the tip of your nose and count each inhale, retention, and exhale to a count of four, measuring the count by your pulse. Do this until you feel that your mind has quieted down considerably (approximately ten minutes).

4. Allow your eyelids to close and your chin to drop slowly until it rests on your chest. Fix your eyes in the third-eye lock position. Feel yourself getting heavier and heavier with each exhale, going deeper and deeper into meditation. Allow yourself to drift downward, to go deeper and become more relaxed. Use the descending count if you like.

5. Do one of the following: repeat a silent mantra over and over (see the list in this chapter) at a rhythm that you find comfortable; do slow hand meditation (see Chapter One); generate the image of a geometric shape (bar, circle, diamond, etc.) and hold it—even a dot of white light will do; do the foaming light exercise in this chapter.

Remain aware of your breathing, especially when you feel that you are involuntarily "coming out" of the meditative state. Make yourself heavier and heavier by adding weight—this is the surest route to a deep meditative state that is both restful and enlightening. Let yourself go, and prepare yourself to observe whatever happens as mere phenomena, not "good" or "bad" occurrences. When images or thoughts come to mind just look at them, let them pass, and return to your relaxation techniques. If you truly do let go, you will relax more deeply and come closer to yourself than you ever have before. Don't worry about "losing" yourself, about having nothing to return to. You can't lose yourself no matter how hard you try. It is *you,* after all, who's doing the meditating!

Self-Exploratory Meditation

It is often interesting and revealing to ask yourself a question when you have arrived in a deep state of meditative equilibrium. You are more open and less defensive in this state than in any other, and consequently more intelligent. Self-remembering in the meditative state can be a rough trip or positively thrilling, and if you're willing to take a few risks and ride the white waters, you may find this exercise of unlimited value.

Direct your questions toward separating what you really know about yourself from your illusions or the illusions and self-deceptions that may have been foisted off upon you by others. Sample questions you might ask yourself (and your subconscious!) follow. When you do this, just ask the question—*don't* try to answer it. Let the answer come to you. Merely ask the question; repeat it like a silent mantra.

1. Who am I?
2. How do I love?
3. What of my parents still lives inside me?
4. What am I afraid of?
5. What would I be like if I were free of fears and anxieties?
6. What do I long for?
7. What should I do to help myself?

Your answers may be disturbing or unexpected, but remember that they come from deep within you while you are in your most open and relaxed state, and they are as close as you can possibly come to what has always been called the truth.

The Meditation of Daily Living

"Never forget . . . yourself."

Tennyson's Method of Meditation

Meditation and altered states of consciousness are certainly not the exclusive province of gurus or movements. Any individual can get the same results independently, on his or her own. William James, in his *Varieties of Religious Experience*, discusses a passage from the memoirs of the poet Alfred Lord Tennyson, who lived long before the days of alpha waves and hundred-dollar mantras.

"I have never had any revelations through anesthetics, but a kind of waking trance—this for lack of a better word—I have frequently had, quite up from boyhood, when I have been all alone. This has come upon me through repeating my own name to myself silently, till all at once, as it were out of the intensity of the consciousness of individuality, individuality itself seemed to dissolve and fade away into boundless being. . . . This [was] not a confused state but the clearest, the surest of the surest, utterly beyond words—where death was an almost laughable impossibility—the loss of personality (if so it were) seeming no extinction, but the only true life. I am ashamed of my feeble description.

Have I not said the state is utterly beyond words?"

Professor Tyndall, in a letter, recalls Tennyson saying of this condition: "By God Almighty! there is no delusion in the matter! It is no nebulous ecstasy, but a state of transcendent wonder, associated with absolute clearness of mind."

Chapter Seven

Sex and Sensory Awareness

YOUR SEXUAL AND SENSUAL LIFE IS ONE IM-
portant area in which the techniques in this book can
create positive change. You can take what you've
learned and apply it to your life as you live it.

In no single area of our lives do armor, energy
blockage, and tension and anxiety play a more oppressive and frustrating role than in sex. Our sexuality
is only a tiny fraction of what it might be, or what it
perhaps once was. Of course, we can trace this pre-
dicament to many social roots and causes—to family
structure, etc.—but the immediate reason that our
sexuality is such a problem is that our bodies are contracted. Sex is a joyous unraveling, and we are tied up
in tight little knots.

All the recent sex research has concluded that sexual problems (even severe sexual dysfunction) are

almost always psychological. That is, they result from anxiety, which is another name for tension. Sex is both cause and effect of a free, high-energy state (good sex equals high energy, and high energy equals good sex), and sex is difficult, if not impossible, in direct proportion to the amount of tension in our bodies. Furthermore, the sexual force in us is suppressed when our minds are preoccupied. If you are unable to relax your body or calm your mind, you will never have the peak sexual experiences that we are all entitled to, that are our birthright.

The orgone energy that Reich postulated (which is the same as Ki, Chi, Prana, *élan vital,* etc.) was actually formulated by him as sex energy. He believed, in other words, that energy was sex and sex was energy, and that the fundamental cause of armor and energy blockage was sexual anxiety. It follows, of course, that if you're able to dissolve armor and raise the level of your energy in general, you're going to raise the level of your sexual energy in particular.

Some of the techniques in this book have a more direct relationship to sexuality than others, and I will now review these techniques and mention others that, modified, can enhance your sex life.

Sex-Related Techniques

Bioenergetic methods—fast breathing in specific poses and the physical expression of repressed angers —are most closely allied to those developed originally by Reich himself, and are definitely liberating for sex. Often, after going through these exercises, you will experience spontaneous sexual arousal. If your sexuality has been waning, bioenergetics is certainly a secret of rejuvenation. And if you wish to increase your powers from a satisfactory level or explore new possibilities in the realm of sexual release, bioenergetics-before-sex is the thing to try.

The **snake** pose from Yoga loosens armor that may inhibit you sexually. Properly done, it will stretch out your neck, spine, chest, diaphragm, belly, and thighs —all the areas that must be mobile and sensitive during sexual activity.

You should follow the snake with the forward-bending **plough.** This, as I mentioned previously, often stimulates you sexually. The reasons for such stimulation are not at all clear, but the exercise's efficacy is undeniable. This pose is also a powerful relaxer and an easy way to clear your mind. (After all, if your mind wanders during sex, pleasure is lost.)

Chest breathing is especially good for releasing sexual energy. Lie on your back and breathe deeply, filling your chest completely. Exhale slowly but vigorously through your mouth, and as you exhale moan forcefully. When you exhale, squeeze all the air from your lungs by contracting the muscles of your chest— squeeze out every last cubic inch. Moan from your chest, not through your nose. Keep your mouth open wide, as if to yawn (if you should break into a spontaneous yawn, that's fine).

As you loosen up, you should feel your moan vibrating in your body at lower and lower levels, until finally it's vibrating your genitals. You may feel that you're getting "carried away" when you do this. Perfect—let it happen. That's precisely the point.

Depending upon what shape your body is in when you begin the exercises in this book, you may find that one or more of the techniques turn you on for no explicable reason. Some people, and I am one of them, even get aroused by certain meditation techniques. Remember which ones get to you, and spend a few moments doing them before you're going to have sex. It will enhance your pleasure immensely.

A couples technique that always works for me is **foot massage.** People are really unaware of the amount of tension that is stored in their feet, and a massage given by your lover will release that tension even more than your own footwork. And foot massage is sexy partly because the feet are such an unattended part of your body that they are really among the most private parts. (Even *you* don't touch them very much.) A foot massage generates a peculiar kind of intimacy because of both the tension release and the private status of feet.

Pay particular attention to the soles of your partner's feet. The idea is not to tickle them, but to really get in deep and *massage* them. Use your thumbs, the heel of your hand, whatever, to dig down and work loose the tension you'll find there. Massage the toes by twirling and squeezing. Do every part of the foot, making sure not to forget the heel, ankle, and lower calf. The soft area on the inside of the foot between ankle and heel should be pressed with the thumb, released, and pressed again a number of times. This area connects via the central nervous system to the genitals.

Don't worry about "not knowing how" to give a foot massage. There's really no great secret to it. You have feet, too. You know what feels good—so do it to your partner. (Your partner, of course, can also tell you what he or she likes.) Just plunge in and massage. You'll get better with practice, and whatever you do can't help but have a good effect.

One caveat: Never, never, never, *never* do just one

foot. Nothing is more frustrating than to be on the receiving end of a one-foot massage. Always do both, or your partner will wind up completely out of equilibrium.

Do your partner's feet first—both of them, of course—and then have your partner do yours. If it feels good, allow yourself to moan and express pleasure. This is both a good release and a way of letting your partner know that he or she is working on the right spot. Don't hesitate to say what you want done, either. As the massage progresses, you'll feel areas that need more work. Say so. Not to say so will only add to the tension and repression you are trying to banish.

Meditation and Sending Energy

There is no reason you can't use meditation and energy-sending techniques to improve your sex life. The idea, of course, is to heighten your sensory awareness—both in your erogenous zones and all over your body (when you become *aware*, you'll be amazed at what odd parts of your body turn out to be erogenous zones!). Through focusing your mind by the techniques you have already learned, you can develop a much higher sensory awareness—you might say you can attain a *super*sensory awareness. Throughout this book I have stressed attention to feeling—physical feeling *and* emotional feeling. In your sex life, feeling is everything.

Try a meditation in which your one-point is your penis or clitoris. The effect, physically and emotionally, can be quite startling. No matter how interested we are in sex, we still tend to hide from a true awareness of our genitals; we refuse to focus on them utterly and completely to see what's really there.

You can also send energy to your genitals. Imagine that the energy concentrated in your mind is flowing down your neck, through your spinal cord, and down into your genitals. With each exhale, send a pulse of energy down this route. Imagine that the route is glowing and electric. Try to actually "see" the pulse of energy flowing from your mind into your sex organs.

You can do these meditations before sex or during sex. The latter will be a fascinating, highly charged experience if both partners are doing it or if you do it alone while masturbating.

A variation you might try is meditation on your skin. Simply go into a meditative state and *feel your skin*. Travel over every inch of it with your mind's eye, make it glow and sparkle, feel how it covers you, feel how you exist inside it, feel how it feels the air and the heat and the cold, even the atmospheric pressure. Feel how your skin is the thing that separates you from external reality and yet, paradoxically, how it is also the very thing that connects you to the outer world. Imagine that all your inner energy is flowing out your skin like glowing steam, and that at the same time your skin is absorbing energy from the atmosphere. Try to *listen* with your skin. Try to guess why animal skins are called "hides."

As you meditate on your skin, have your partner touch it, lightly at first, everywhere. Be prepared for sensations of pleasure you never imagined possible. (Make sure you are well into the meditative state before you do this if you want it to work well.) For an extra thrill, meditate on your skin as you do chest breathing and moaning.

Meditative Sex

This style of lovemaking is used in the ancient ritual practices of (Tibetan) Tantric Yoga and, incidentally or coincidentally, as a sexual therapy for the anxious patients of Masters and Johnson. If you have fears about reaching orgasm, reaching orgasm too soon, or reaching orgasm too late, or if you wish to get more from sex than a ten- or twenty-minute pop of pleasure, you'll like meditative sex. It makes sex far more beautiful and lasting, deeper, more rich and savory in the small pleasurable details.

First, restrict your foreplay so that neither you nor your partner are allowed to touch the other's genitals. Spend your time on the other, little-known and little-explored erogenous zones: the neck, elbows, stomach, knees, feet, flanks, armpits, scalp, temples, gums, etc. When your entire body (and your partner's) has been awakened over every inch and your genitals cannot bear being ignored any longer—when you've really gone past your level of tolerance and then gone past it once again—you may include the genitals in your foreplay.

Do not allow the genital eroticism to go on too long. As soon as you can do so, establish penetration.

Both of you should focus all your mental energy on the genitals during and after penetration. Leave the rest of your body to its own devices and disappear inside your penis or vagina until your entire consciousness fills your sex organs.

Do not initiate the customary rhythmic thrusting motions of ordinary sex. Keep your motions gentle and subtle. If you can, keep still entirely. Create a unity of deep breathing with your partner, so that you are both inhaling and exhaling at the same time.

The idea in meditative sex is twofold: One, to remain in the sexual embrace as long as possible *without orgasm,* and two, to meditate continuously upon your sex organs as a one-point, with no other thought in your mind.

Feel the warmth, the juices, the flesh upon flesh, the effect on your total body, everything. Remember, the idea is a minimum of movement and a totality of concentration upon vagina and penis with no other thoughts in the mind—and *no orgasm.*

Meditative sex can last for several hours, and, if you really allow yourself to experience it without rushing toward the mandatory orgasm, you will experience a new relation to your sexual self. You will feel sexual energy coming in powerful waves, retreating, coming in waves again, retreating again. Your lips may become pleasantly "numb," and you may see colors dancing in the darkness. The tactile sense in your fingers increases tremendously.

After a few hours of this, or at least an hour, you may feel that it's time to have an orgasm—or you may be thoroughly satisfied without one. You *will* see, for certain, that orgasm is not the defining feature of sex, and that whether it happens quickly or late is not nearly as important an issue as it is usually made out to be. The important thing is the generation of love energy.

If you do decide to have an orgasm, try to determine *afterward* whether it enhanced or damaged your energy state—it can work one way for some people and the other way for others, and may work differently for the same person in different instances. Remember that to note the ramifications of energy states you should not look merely to the few minutes after sex, but to a day later or even more.

Try meditative sex with a terminal orgasm and without, seeking the different effects. You may decide you want *both* to become a part of your sex life, depending upon your needs at varying times.

Meditation on Sex

One of the critical mechanisms of sexual repression is the occupation of our minds by thoughts or emotions "deliberately" designed by the subconscious to mask our sexual feelings. In a way it's a good thing, since without repression we might always be horny and unable to even walk down the street without making love to two or three passersby. Of course we can't be quite that primitive in the world we live in, but we can increase the level of our sexual interest to one that is more natural. We can be a little less repressed without destroying the fabric of our lives or of society.

One good way to lift this veil of repression about things sexual is to meditate on the abstract subject of sex, or on concrete sexual images.

To meditate on the subject of sex in general, enter a meditative state by means of one of the techniques described in the previous chapter. When you have reached a deep and quiet level, ask yourself some crucial question about sex. How do I feel about sex? What do I do to avoid my feelings about sex? How did my parents feel about sex? How does my own attitude reflect sentiments acquired from my parents? How does my usual partner feel about sex? What would sex be like for me if it were different and better? What do I feel in the moments just before sex? Just after? What *is* sex, after all?

When you ask yourself one of these questions, just ask it. Don't try to formulate an answer or think it through; that will get you nowhere. You must ask the question and then wait *passively* for an answer or part of an answer to come to you. Sometimes you'll draw a blank—if you do, don't strain for more than your subconscious is willing to yield up; just go to another question. You are looking for your very deepest, truest feelings, not for what you "know," and these truest feelings can come to you spontaneously from the levels of mind below consciousness. You are, you might say, your own crystal ball. Sometimes all is clear and illuminating; sometimes it's just a milky opaqueness. Often the answers you receive will be difficult to face and hard to swallow. So, don't swallow them! Spit them out, spit them out as fast as you can—all the way out of your system.

If you don't like something about yourself, there's no law that says you must resignedly accept it as a "part" of you. Sexual hangups are weeds overgrowing the mind. When you locate them precisely, in meditation, you have a chance to start afresh. It's like creating a garden. Once you pull out the weeds and cultivate the soil, all you have to do is check up now and then to make sure no weeds are growing back. You *do* have a chance to start anew, but you need to be brave. You have to start acting from "want" instead of "should."

To make sex a more integral part of your consciousness and to get rid of some of the heavy weeds of repression that are slowly choking it out, spend some time meditating upon a sexual image. This might be your partner—naked, masturbating, making love to you—an ideal partner ("the most beautiful" or "the most handsome"), an image of disembodied genitals, an image from a movie or book, or even an image of yourself making love in some forbidden situation (with your boss, or parent, or mailman, or maid). Whatever, as they say, turns you on.

This meditation should not be confused with mere fantasy. Here, you go into a deep state and consciously focus your attention on a sexual image for the express purpose of releasing yourself from sexual repression. Over a period of time, you will see that meditation on sex has precisely this effect. Mere fantasy, however, is unguided and undirected. Fantasy only *reflects* the state of repression and inhibition in an individual—it doesn't change anything. However, you might effectively take an image from one of your fantasies and explore it deeply, make *use* of it, during a meditation on sex.

Breathing and Sex

Since energy is at its peak during an exhale, any sexual movement, or movement during sex, will have its effect enhanced and increased if it is performed during an *exhale*. (Recall the holding of the breath leading up to orgasm, then the great and primeval *exhale*.)

Slow Motion and Sex

Slowness creates heightened sensation and response. It works on the body and the mind at the same time. No one truly interested in sex should neglect spending at least a portion of lovemaking time in *infinitely slow* activity. *Infinitely* slow. Sex is a real tortoise-and-the-hare situation. Slow but sure definitely wins the "race."

The Trembling Orgasm

The non-genital orgasm, orgasm-without-coming, is one of the most fascinating and least-known experiences in sex. Not everyone will be able to have this unique kind of orgasm, but when you get really loose and turned onto your body, you can. One wonderful feature of the non-genital orgasm is that there is no limit to the number you can have in one love-making session, whether you are a man or a woman. Another is that this orgasm *always* makes you more relaxed—it never dissipates energy. It's not as overwhelming or total an experience as the orgasm that we ordinarily think of, but the two by no means exclude each other, and you can easily have both.

Have your partner begin to masturbate you. Allow your entire body to move freely in response to your partner's caresses. When your sexual excitement begins to reach a peak, allow your body to begin contracting as if you were coming to orgasm. (You can give the process a little push by slightly tensing the muscles of your upper abdomen, near the solar plexus, and drawing your chin forward in a little jerk.) Before climax, when you begin to tremble, your partner should stop caressing and just touch your penis or clitoris gently. Then, using your powers of concentration, disperse the energy from your genitals to your chest and limbs, exhaling sharply. Allow the trembling to build and build in momentum until finally it is strong enough to take control, to tremble on and on, carrying you away in its motion. Continue to tremble as long as it lasts. Don't cut it short. (One always has a tendency to cut surprise experiences short.)

The more trembling orgasms you have, the more open your body will become, and the more magnificent will be your final, conventional, purely sexual orgasm(s).

Dissolving Inhibitions—The Idea of Voluptuousness

The anxieties and physical tensions that occur in us during sex represent boundaries beyond which we cannot go—or beyond which we find ourselves in areas where fear severely restricts our enjoyment and pleasure. These boundaries are demarcated by what we call *inhibitions*. Our inhibitions are *in*-us prohibitions; we often try to externalize them by saying we "shouldn't" do this or that, or such-and-such is "not nice," or "gross," or "animal," but in fact inhibitions are, by definition, always internal and imaginary.

The causes of inhibition are manifold. Since there is neither time nor space here to delve into the roots of every inhibition, suffice it to say that our total society is inhibited, and it creates individuals who are inhibited in kind.

Until very recently (and the remains of the past are still very much with us), our society in general—reinforced by parents, institutions, and popular art forms—had a single and definitive reply to strongly felt sexuality or sensuality. The reply was NO.

But you can say, from the deepest center of yourself, YES. You can confirm the undeniable fact that you are an animal that lives, breathes, lusts, squirms, and feels as well as a human that thinks. You can cease the repression of your sensuous nature and say, in contradiction of the outmoded mores of our Puritan-founded country, that to *feel,* emotionally and physically, is good and right—and that without such feeling, you cannot be real.

The forces opposing eroticism and sensuality are at work in all of us. The great task of the maturing and independent individual is to perceive those forces in him- or herself, and to counter those forces with an affirmation of inner life and energy, of fluid and motile existence free from the fetters of repression.

When we are happy, we always *feel* good. Whether it is brought on by the breath of fresh air in the country or the scent of roses in a small city apartment, happiness is almost always accompanied by a sensuous arousal. To make *all* life more attractive and to insure a continuous happiness within yourself, you have got to permit your innate voluptuousness to burst into colorful bloom. You must *permit* yourself to feel good, to *love* feeling good, to glory in sexy or sensuous sensations, to flow with them and glide in their currents, to let your sensuous nature take you wherever it wants to go—to let it take you back to your own nature and the sights, sounds, touches, colors, tastes, aromas, and vibrations of nature itself.

Voluptuousness need not be a moment you experience once or twice in lapses of heady abandon. It can be a way of existing in the world, in every instant and detail of your life. Slow down. Hear the richness of all the melodies around you in every harmonic note. Smell the soil in your potted plants or in your yard. Touch your face—it's very smooth. Taste every food as if for the first time. You'll be in for a constant stream of surprises and delights. Little things will become far more beautiful and lovely than big things. You will bring yourself into the present, into the time and space in which you actually live.

And remember, no matter how much you feel that they are "right" and that you want to defend and support them, your inhibitions have been dropped into you and spread inside you like a drop of India ink in a glass of pure water. Your inhibitions are *not you*—they're alien. And no matter how much you want to defend an inhibition, you should keep in mind that it is limiting your life. It is making you, even if in the smallest way, less than you are, other than who you are, less than you could be. Be brave. An inhibition is only as strong as you imagine it to be. Relax—and by now you know how—and your fears will relax with you, into nothingness. As you relax you will become more beautiful physically. You will *feel* more beautiful, the world will *appear* more beautiful, and sex and sensuality will arise within you as a reward that all the money on earth cannot buy.

Chapter Eight

How and When to Practice

IN YOUR DAILY LIFE, CHOOSE THE TECHNIQUES that you like best and do them whenever you can. You can do breathing and relaxation exercises *anytime* you're not involved in a social situation. You can do them while riding in a car, bus train, or plane, while standing in line, while waiting for an appointment. You can do movement techniques while walking or during a break in study or office routine. The same goes for the still-life methods. Sex, of course, has its own times and places.

It's good if you can have a workout or a special session once a day, even if only for fifteen minutes. Choose the exercises you like best and that work best for you, and do them (for best results) in the following sequence:

1. breathing
2. still life
3. movement
4. breathing
5. meditation and deep relaxation

A strict program could be set up that would tell you to do this, then do that, then do that and that, but it would miss the key point of this book. There are *many* ways to become relaxed and energized. Different ways will work for different people, or even for the same person at different times. So treat this book as a smorgasbord, going from appetizers to desserts, in order, loading up on whatever catches your fancy. If you give yourself a session once a day, or even several times a week, you will virtually guarantee yourself positive inner change. You'll be more relaxed, have more energy, and have a freer mind, a happier soul, stronger passion—all the things that make life worth living.